Selected Poems

By the same author

Living Room
From the Other Country
Over the Wall
Out for the Elements

Compiled and introduced by Andrew Waterman

The Poetry of Chess

ANDREW WATERMAN

Selected Poems

CARCANET

For my son, Rory, towards whom these poems grow, who will grow towards them.

Acknowledgements
Acknowledgements are due to the editors of the following, in which most of the new poems written since those in my last book have appeared: *Critical Quarterly, Encounter, Literary Review, London Magazine, PN Review, Some Contemporary Poets of Britain and Ireland.*

First published in Great Britain 1986 by
Carcanet Press Ltd
208-212 Corn Exchange Buildings
Manchester M4 3BQ

The publisher acknowledges the financial assistance of the Arts Council of Great Britain

British Library Cataloguing in Publication Data

Waterman, Andrew

Selected poems.
I. Title
821'.914 PR6073.A823

ISBN 0-85635-668-9

Typeset by Bryan Williamson, Swinton, Berwickshire
Printed in England by Short Run Press, Exeter

Contents

The Song

She sang the song the Belgian refugees
brought to the valley's mills in the Great War.
Straight in his narrow chair her husband sat,
blending a phrase. They were young then.

Their young have gone away. When her eyes went
he sold the weaver's-cottage, brought her down
to the terrace in the Bottom, fixed downstairs
for her wheelchair: bedroom, bath, no doors.

He does the women's work, and washes her.
When relatives call she talks of the old view
from home up on the Edge – moor, clough and sky.
But massive today in a darkening brown room

she sings the strange French words the Belgians taught her,
as if the mind's lens pours all summers since
back on one blot of light. She was young then,
the foreign music was the outside world.

Charged with its resonance the flowered teaset
on the Welsh dresser is set vibrating:
speckless teapot, milk-jug, rows of cups
she kept for best, and never filled or drank from.

Death in the Valley

So it came to this:
the years of grit, of being
"beholden to no-one"
contracted to a room,

her husband's farmer-hulk
dumped on a couch dying,
herself near-blind, arthritic,
still keeping the place tidy.

From the black mill-villages
clinging below the moorland
relatives call, take tea,
in the glow of the hearth and polished

surfaces and shining
brass and copper things
watch the brawn hand twitching
at nothing, on the coverlet.

"Nurse says he'll not last weekend."
They talk of their own ailments.
On the mantelpiece, beneath
three plaster flying ducks,

him in his striped demob-suit
that week they had in Blackpool,
and donkeys, and the children.
Who now in distant cities

reading "I can't write more.
I'm not myself since Father
passed on. But I manage,"
are steadied with a sense

of a lifetime's cramped persistence
dying in slow pieces,
leaving a world tidy
they'll not go back to live in.

A Landscape for Edward Thomas

Journeying often across the heart of England,
Oxford to Leicester, I watched winter
exacting frankness as it stripped a landscape
rain-sodden in early-failing light:
iron ploughland glinting, sheep
shorn of complacency, the air absorbing
colour or dazzle, sopping up all contrast.

Sad November trees scattered along
the level fields fling bare branches entreating
nothing, for nothing particular,
no gift of bud or birdsong on one bough
could signify: joy in this grey season
would be disease. Austerely all
endures until some general change of climate,
astonishing, perhaps to come, but not
absolving from responsibility
to what exists, is possible, today.
Pools sprawled down long troughs in fields reflect
blankly the sky's wide openness.

The unforgotten pretensions summer flourished,
its foliate rhetoric, saturated, numbed
with richness, certainties. But this meagre landscape
could draw a scrutiny that refuses
the accomplishment of gesture to reach through
submission to the strictness of what is
the finer truths there resonant, alert
to chips of flint, splashes of dung
feigning white flowers of spring, even
when it is spring, in solitude
drenched clean as earth by rain, still travelling on
down green roads, disused possibilities
long overgrown that yield an intimate
voice hinting from past the edge of the world
inhuman harmonies through a bird's song,
seeking beyond where it could last turn back.

Mother

I should be grateful. You
adopted me in a hard time,
the sound of guns from Dunkirk shaking
London, the bombs. You have told
how once you lay over my pram as a German
aeroplane swooped to machine-gun the street.
What made you, you never did say.

It was only "You should be grateful" became
the theme you played on a subtle keyboard
(you'd not been an actress in vain):
grateful for supper, for half-days in Brighton,
for wellington boots in rainy weather,
"For all I have done for you."
There was also your tone saying "Don't."

And when father left you said nothing,
except – remember? – when
I finally asked, that day in the park
at the rusted green cafeteria seats,
to distract me, "Look at those sparrows,"
and did not notice rage boiling the dregs
of a nine-year-old's childhood away.

So I locked you from me in turn, as I locked
my schoolwork away in a case.
Where was I going? "Out."
And when leaving for good I came
to tell you, you carried on hanging up washing,
not taking the peg from your mouth just said
"Remember to leave your doorkey."

At seventy now, arthritis
has withered the touch and range
from your piano-player's hands,
your first teeth are gone (years after mine).
Hoarding a fossil faith

in Stalin, the god that failed,
you keep up the garden, read Dickens, see plays,

and we can be easier together,
and I am truly grateful.
If what you pinched and scraped once seemed
me, I know now it was for me,
understand things you still cannot say
as your talkative letters come, each signed
not "with love," just "as ever".

from *"Railway Poems"*

II
Night Worker

Jacko's been on straight nights twenty year.
He's got that pale look. No-one envies him.
In winter, never sees the sun except
weekends. You don't sleep right, the traffic, heat,
playground noises, doorbells, hammerings, light
fluttering the curtains. Then it's up at five,
supper for breakfast, pints and darts, till clocking-
on, and foreman's yell, "Let's have yer then."
Twenty year! Why even yet, at three,
when he's had his snap, head's down on messroom table.
The body never adjusts. Or when the shunt's
not up, nowt's doing, he'll stretch out beat on sacks.
Nights isn't natural.
                                    And yet he'll talk
of how the city looks at dead of night
as he smokes a crafty fag by the Humberstone wall
after the street-lamps go out, houses, shops
unearthly like, and it's all stars; or how
moths brush his cheeks out down the running roads;
how dawn comes up behind the Grain Shed, grey
or pearl, air stirring, cool light striking from
odd angles on wet slates; and going home
from barrer-running crates of fruit, the only
man in a bus against the rush, his pockets
stuffed with apples, straw stuck on his boots.

Weekends, he keeps indoors and watches telly
uses his holidays doing-up the house.

VI
A Butterfly

Even under the shed there's something outdoors
about the work. One side stands open

to stars and wind. You pause on your barrow to watch
dawn come up, or a shower across the city.

You're never bricked in. On slack shifts in summer
men wander off along overgrown sidings, embankments,

for a sun and a glance through the *Mirror*: a couple
have planted a vegetable-garden back of Humberstone Coal Wharf.

Grass invades. Dustiest corners are settled
with unauthorised flowers. The Grain Shed sparrows

strut plundering leaking sacks, great rats
buck-jump away from right under your feet.

On a fine day wagons trundle in hung with glittering
waterdrops: somewhere rain is falling.

Even one bleak night, surrounded
by foggy blackness, and cartons, crates,

rolls of netting stacked up on the shed-platform,
hard graft, something broke in when old Gumble found

in the straw that wadded a cased-up carboy of acid
a sleepy butterfly. It crawled

on to his palm. "Beautiful little bugger,
in't it?" It fluttered in his sour beer breath.

"Look at this, Jacko. Red Admiral." Wherever
he carried it, cupped precious in his hands,

men stopped, gathering under wan lights:
blue overalls, stubbled faces focused on

a butterfly, straw strewn upon the concrete,
and birds starting racketing for the new day in the girders.

VII
Harry

Harry came on the Railways before the war.
Stable boy. Small enough to duck under
the horse's belly for lifting up the hoofs.
His soft voice dwells like a gloss on the "hosses":
"They were lovely. Human really. You'd talk to them.
They knew you. All had their own personalities.
Some were that vicious, kicking and bucking,
they couldn't be harnessed, or stealthy like, when you went
in to sweep shit and mush they'd close up and roll you over
on stable floor. Couldn't take some of them near
a dray-load of carrots, they'd clean it out.
They weren't scrawny buggers, the railway hosses,
plenty of meat on them. They took prizes. We'd deck them
in red and blue ribbons for the May Day parades.
You could take a pride in the hosses,
not like these cabs they brought in in 'fifty-one.
More reliable, too, give a hoss a bag of hay,
he'd go all day. Them buggers always break down."

On the night fire gutted the old Bell Lane stables, Harry
couldn't watch. He walked off, his limp worse than usual
from the foot a bay trod on, smashed twenty years back.

XI
The Inmates

Some, one can't imagine outside the yard.
Dwarfed by the draughty Victorian sheds
they break down into their work.

The machinery, leaky hydraulic hoists,
splintered turntables embossed 1860,
frayed ropes, rusted tackle, bent crowbar,

unites with limps, maimed hands, greasy caps
grown to pulverised faces sporting
Sellotaped Health Service specs, pink and white

wobbly false teeth, in a slow
organic deterioration. When not in use
they'll stand propped on wonky barrows till grass

comes up through their boots. A blowlamp would hardly
flake off soiled layers of clothing. Leisure
is sprawling on rotten casks

beneath weak lighting that yellows the skin,
sunning where a south wall holds the heat,
on a fine day pottering cuttings blackberrying;

in little huts scattered among the wilderness
of tracks they settle into a sludge
of used rosters, racing-sheets, calendars.

Red jelly one night in a washroom basin
meant Snowy'd gone after forty years: "haemorrhage".
The Railways had finished him off.

Bury his frame in Hoss Dock under
old sleepers, or let it rest in long grass
out of foreman's road back of the Grain Shed

till rank flowers sprout through his eyes, *Reveille*
folded over his knees, enamel
tea-mug gripped in skeleton hand.

Solstice

Waking into
the landscape of my heart
it is snow.

Contours have
slipped. The loss of bearings
unfocuses me

and slopes I relied on
just being there firm
in every season

to pour
me back into myself
are blanked away.

Stumbling for paths
no earthly spring can find
I fall locked

into a backward
dream freezing a valley
all blossom and shade.

Hands

It is the hands
live on. I watch
wonderingly out of
the skull's shell

their slow underwater
tensionings wring
suds through a shirt,
their firm grasp

to puncture a can
of coffee releasing
the fresh aroma.
Peeling an orange

or in a mirror
knotting my tie
they flex intricately
like animate things.

How peaceably now
they rest, lightweight
on knees, blue-veined,
dusted with hair,

before moving
unfalteringly on
to construct the spare
scaffolding of deed

assuring tomorrow.
They dress me to meet it;
record on this page
its intimations.

The Dream

We'd hurt each other. Now I sat alone
drowsing on hot carriage-cushion where
along Lough Foyle the Derry train drifts wide
of anything like land: ribbed sand
ribboned and glazed with water mirrors sky
and the seagull's loop: which real, which mirage?

And it seemed you were with me: I said,
"A dream-blend of all elements – like peace."
And outside the window a gull stilled
wings unmoving – or was it the train that stilled?

Beyond blue sea in which light steadied to
a million points, lay cloud-soft Donegal;
the other way, a sort of green fen spread,
trees, hedges, cattle in long grass, white stone –
the only movement bounding hares –
then suddenly Benevenagh's reared head,
sun picking out the topmost weave of grass.

"No," you said. "It is no dream, but life –
beautiful things, but you must glimpse them while
they're in your vision, you can't stop the train."

"I am on the train too, we move together."

The gull had fallen back, the glinting peak
receded. Then you screamed,
flung the compartment-door wide, jumped, were gone.

At least, I was on my own when the train pulled in
through wharves, warehouses, Derry's rank black walls.

Living Room

Once, a bare room, a sill
to lean from. Easy, when spring
took the streets with a simmer of blossom
and roofgutter sparrows wrung
from themselves ever fresher song,
to pack up and go.

Now seasonable lusts,
regrets, again infest
the blood like viruses,
I keep indoors, although
out on the common, grass
bursts through dumped chairs, stoves, cars.

Freedom to thrust like that
through all I've dumped into
a bare life since first bareness
seemed failure forfeited
by each act that furnished it,
I dwell here claimed by what
I've chosen: living room
that by the more it holds
feels less my home.

Summer 1970

It is the season of death,
furred, feathered things crushed to the roads,
insects smacking themselves
to pulp on the windscreen, and
the bulldozer gouging back
ditch, hedgerow, root and branch:
gashed green bleeds red soil.
"Community Relations Committee
campaigns to keep temperature down":
but in town after little town
strident with union jacks
riding its fields afloat
on tidal flute and drum
the heat beats up. The road
dips from the hills into
the hazed pit of Belfast,
an army-truck gouts black smoke
over late-flowering thorn;
the sniper climbs to his roof,
wall blazoned "One man one gun".

Moontrips

Beyond our local roofs, unfocused streets,
rises the moon, the poets', lovers' moon,
and now the scientists', who also go
awkward for something elemental there:
touching empiricists with scoops and tapes
collecting data, they may turn
back all-American eyes and see amazed
our coloured globe harmoniously spin whole.

Life-support systems cannot long sustain
unearthly visions. Gravity compels
re-entry through polluted atmosphere,
touchdown. They vanish back
into the piecemeal of a daily world,
that peering close-up struggles to make what
it may of what's been gathered: moon-dust, rocks,
grey shards of the ineffable.

Not that one can go back

Not that one can go back and start again.
Perhaps, to a blue garden gate,
the momentary bloom of sunshine mute upon
pavement dust, dusty leaves, red pillarbox,
the pebbledashed house where my mother hoarded her worries.
"I'm going to quit school. And home," I told a friend,
spinning my bicycle wheel till it kindled a blaze.

Or later, the river at Richmond, night:
against the dark flood a swan held its place and its poise,
neck arched, possibility questing.
"Marry me," I said. She did. And that went wrong.

And elsewhere, to another, "We'd best part."

What is cast off, and what is taken on –
living, one acts from doubt, the contradictions
never resolve for waiting; and not to trust
those special moments when something blossoms, or rides
a rising tide, is the greatest sin;
not less because sun is just sunny, and swan swan.

And yet, "There is something inherently mean in action,"
Coleridge says; and I think of how each deed
destroys its alternatives; how most of pain
is burying them; and of this dream:
outside in a lightless street I am prising open
a drain. There issues a sulphurous underground smell.
And I lift out one by one translucent sopping
murdered embryos; heap them in the gutter.
A silent crowd has gathered. I cannot see
their faces. I know I am guilty.

Not that one can go back and start again.

The Two Roads

The fork in the path
came up before
I was ready to choose;
I found I had taken
the sky road. At first
I could glimpse through thicket
the other lane dipping,
escorted by water,
between flowering banks,
rollered lawns, white stone dwellings.
A turn lost the view.
And what with the rain
closing in, the unsheltered
climbing a stony
road riding blown grass,
it was only attaining
the ridge I could look
down through snatches of cloud
at the coast road whole:
past meadows where cows
stood in clusters it followed
the strand to the bay's
bluest haven, a house,
sunlit garden, child playing
as if who belonged there
might have been me;
who appearing now
did not look up,
would be deaf at such distance
to the nothing I knew
was all I could say now.

Calling

I took it in when I first called to view,
through-traffic slushing beneath a railbridge,
peeling shopfronts, lustreless shut pubs,
a yard full of scrapped trolleybuses, dead
antennae aimless under a grey sky,
somewhere behind, the river,
and the street I sought off-left, cracked pavement,
gardens all weeds, the odd house boarded up.
After knocking, I turned in the pause:
across the road an open window framed
a headscarved woman moving, dusting, singing.
The massive pink door shuddered to let me in.
And I was led up past landing kitchenettes,
and round and up to a slope-roofed room, low bed,
bed-table, tilting wardrobe, cheap bowl fire.
"That's it, and there's the meter." Then,
"You're young," he added, "where is your home?"
"Home?" I replied. "Home's where I find myself."

And so it was. Perhaps I have never left.
Coming round different corners since
I am caught surprised by a different door, red, blue,
wrong to my expectation of that blistering pink one,
and the strange accents of a different now;
my silences reassume the network
of those streets, whatever noise traffic makes
modulates to their noise; imagination
attunes to that cramped box. Which first
wrung notes towards what it had for song from it;
where I settled for what calling found me.

Gardens

"This is your garden. Dig it."
Eight hummocky feet by three in a rancid corner.
Bored, I poked about, chopped at worms, bought seeds

at Woolworth's in vividly illustrated packets.
Such as came up looked shoddier, or were just weeds.
And besides, I preferred running off down the forest.

Since then I've had no gardens, "And no regrets,"
I usually say, "they enslave you."
All those bank-clerks pruning their privet each Sunday!

Not but what peering in on some shimmering lawn
with water-sprinklers rotating for ever, splodged
with immaculate flowerbeds, there's not envy –

though the silver-haired bloke at the roller framed against
open french windows is not my style,
nor such casual-seeming perfectedness, not to mention

rustic bird-baths, phoney tudor lanterns.
Still, as I move on, does the wrought-iron of his gate
bar his world or mine? I wonder.

And I quite like to haunt public gardens;
or those of stately homes, with statuary,
ornamental cascades and grottoes, hedges cut

into classically soluble mazes,
or some landscaped romantic vista along a lake,
trees shovelled up into the clouds.

And back looking out of whatever rooms I've got
at some rubbly yard with bins, or untended jungle
where you hear the tumbledown walls' stones grinding in frost

I hanker after illusive gardens,
from Adam and Eve to *Alice*; and that one
in the story everyone's read, through a magical gate

in a wall in a drab city street.
Some fertile green congruence: I can almost feel
its moss, catch scents in the breeze, hear the sound of water.

"Concrete the bloody things over and leave yourself free."
Yet now, if I found myself settling for one,
I'd set about digging.

Intimation

"Aunt Ginnie's dead." Aunt Ginnie's dead. The words
stilled a garden, butterfly in mid-loop,
each leaf and bird, the cherry petals fluttering
down, the child with cup held waiting.

Until his father came down from the loft,
reading the telegram walked out with his mother.
And the world rolled on. The sparrows ate the crumbs,
flew off, were eaten; leaves browned, trembled, fell,

and were replaced by leaves. And I am here,
my mother there, my father elsewhere. Something
holds, like a photograph; rather, a landscape
I find myself re-entering unprepared.

The child, focused on some far point, is blank
to me, the ground he'll cross to where I see him from:
him, a butterfly slipped from time's arc,
and the dropped cup no more blossom will be saved in.

from *"Epilogues"*

1. *Household*

Names on the bellpush labels change
by the month; the house remains:
asymmetrical in rank garden
where nothing is tended but washing,
and a lurching pear-tree
still showers petals on grass,
worn wall, crazed path.
The iron gate hangs unhinged.

Tenants, not speaking
even goodmornings, edge past
on landings, behind partitions
listen to one another's private sounds;

share only dustbins,
front steps kept by two pedestalled
stone lions, doggish and bird-dunged,
a thin pulse of tune from separate radios,
and a roof still crowning
all with a prodigal eccentricity:
green dome, castellations, turrets,
and a railed platform high for stargazing
Victorian paterfamilias, who kept
a home together.

3. *Answer*

A single garden of roses, thickly wrought
red roses hoarding sun in the silence
of a low blind street end-on to a warehouse wall,
scheduled for clearance.
                                        Blistering paint,

broken panes, the other small plots abandoned
to weeds, dropped tiles, gaped blank to what
had determined this immaculate aftermath.

Red blooms. Soft-burning still in vivid answer.

4. *Hymns*

I

Dropped stucco, boarded
windows, aimlessly
spiralling dust,
one creaking shop-blind.
A lamp shattered by
the casual stone
arches an upstairs
window, sashed-high,
where a headscarved woman
moves dusting, singing:
". . . through pastures green
He leadeth me
the quiet waters
by." One street,
one minute attuned
to impossible music.

II

Sudden access
of light, and green
sparking along
boughs lopped in winter
come painfully always;
a brilliant rush
that stuns itself now
into perfect stillness:
white blossom calms
the street, foot falls

steadily upon pavement,
a bird rings one note
on the sky's pure bowl;
we promise, we promise,
ingathered to a moment
helplessly credible; already blurring.

III

An ice-cream van's chime
from parched suburb aspiring
trembles in blue air,
like seaweed in water.

6. *Last Fruit*

Planted behind today's houses
are fruit-trees spaced to a more lavish scale
ghosting the definitions of gardens
belonging to homes now gone.

Replaced by twenties villas,
mock-tudor semis, last season's box of flats:
high-density discord superimposing
tight limits out back.

And rooted where they always were, the trees'
disposition misses some lawns; while some
have apple-tree, pear or plum,
fruits for the picking.

With age, the yields are lessening:
branches fail, are lopped; and then the trunk,
to a stump good only for bowling at;
till hacked out and burnt.

Meanwhile, still lucky children
can play catching fluttering blossom in a cup;
and stray out on a frosty dawn
for the last windfall.

Great Blasket

From land's extremity the island
entices, delectable with shadow.

The landing-place is clefted between rock,
and a green road loops up

around what have been dwellings: roofless,
foundering into blown grass set

with flower-constellations I have no name for.
Elemental enough: some sheep, the sea

they rode in curraghs casting nets;
the long winters of inbred storytelling

in the Irish; the young drifting to mainland
jobs and marriages. Till all were taken off.

And if this twenty-year dereliction harboured
ghosts, there'd be nothing to be said

except agreement how across the water
always looked more alluring.

The boat collects us. From the stern
I see, before a shower cuts off, the broken

walls still marking each frail holding,
a longer stay than mine, and not romantic.

An Ulster Garland

Close by my kitchen window juts
a wall, rich-textured, scarred
brickwork of ochre, grey and red
many times cemented, showing
faint whitewash from before
the house was last patched up.
And where the roof of split slates slopes
to its corner has somehow taken
root among fissures a sprig
of wallflowers, arching
luminous now in the late sunshine.

Delicate, the flowers
have survived nights, and many downpours,
found sustenance amid crumbling.
I have come to expect them.

No, they would not, should it come,
prevail against bulldozer, or bomb;
nor admit their relevance.
And should these petals be torn by explosion,
buried deep under rubble, so
each unique thing must be lost, and is
irrevocable; yet always

others continue, reappear
contriving such root somewhere, so
configured on moving skies.

I drop my gaze on close
unfocused roofline ridges set
at jarring angles.
                    This
is Ireland now, where mobs command
and kill, and terror grips.
"The power system is at breakdown point."

Lightless, I look
again for the yellow flowers upon
their brink; also remark
among the streets' cross-hatching sprays
of answering greenery, deepening
as day ebbs; in low
untended yards, how cranesbill, vetch,
sweetrocket, speedwell, flowers
run wild I have no name for,
sustain their points of colour; and grass
persists, unorganised. By kind
pervasive to outlast
what coming darkness.

26 MAY 1974

Summer Truce

The weather holds. From Strangford Lough to Swilly
soft arms of coast cradle still water.
Sunning before our shore's-edge cottage we
"enjoy it while it lasts", watch floated fronds
of seaweed among the rocks slightly
lifting with a glitter like broken glass.

And the radio talks into blue day –
to campions, sea-pinks, primroses run wild
over springy turf – of another sectarian killing,
a club blown up, several injured.
The tiny insistent voice is a black mote
in the mind, troubling the horizon

within which our concerns are local as
the cliff-path hesitating its few miles
to Portrush. We have our jokes, lovemaking,
morning-squabbles; John and Mary are at
each other's throats in phone-kiosks, kitchens;
another friend founders in private madness;

and "Fuck off to Limavady" as the man said
last night to his girl, means over the edge
of the little world. But later ourselves beyond
Limavady, we find in Derry
the truce keeps up, with festive bunting and
the soldiers relaxed and eating ice-cream.

We drink campari in sweet evening air
where mountains pour down to the lough-side;
seething at Reggie you shred a pound note with your teeth.
– And this morning sit writing it up in your journal
here on the city wall, where ten days back
that policeman was shot from no personal anger.

All peace is imperfect. At last Belfast: the pub
where we talk poetry is pocked from old bombings –
nothing's worth fixing these days. In the gents'
a washbasin grimed and fractured, filled with glass,
taps issuing only a parched gush of air.
Outside, still sunshine. Everyone waits for the break.

1975

From Ireland

Green from Ireland,
and a childhood of pushing prams, –
I can imagine your fireship innocence.

You danced all night,
telling them all the ways their lives were wrong;
kept up in London like treading water.

Now, grounded here, you laugh
at yourself then – until you gasp, as if
roots stirred with a sharp pain

for all that laughter is a loosening from:
home; a confirmation gown;
the holy candles of the faithful poor.

Hiatus

Departure comes as a relaxing; sheds
along the wharves leak light, and gemlike
lamps squander across black water,
orange and white flakes spending to darkness;
hulls and gantries ghost a formal stillness
passing, and the recessive land
is pricked as with minute abandoned faces.

The last buoy winks, the lough expands
to the steady rock and rock of open sea,
and companioned only by the wave-skipping moon
I, the woman profiled against a hatchway,
the crowd in the bar, are cradled weightless,
lives transfused by the throbbing of the engines.

Tomorrow, the glittering rail
where screaming gulls pluck bread, the scattering
knock upon a different shore
luminous with the new day's compulsions.

Peanuts in Troy

"That a man should live on peanuts in a town called Troy!" –
Gissing, in *New Grub Street*. Which, with night,
and the whisper of traffic on wet roads,
conjures that single room back, the ceiling
with its Africa-shaped dampstain sloped so close
you couldn't sit up in bed. I lay
late-burning my high light, while far below
rain like an expensive firework was falling
golden past streetlamps.

Those were the bread and peanut butter days;
one hard week, just ginger biscuits
I especially disliked, bought so they would last.
But the scraps such solitude feasted on:
caught gestures glimpsed through panes, cries from the street;
a bobbing orange umbrella that floated up
through my consciousness like a bubble to break,
its fallout sifting to my notebooks, scarred tin ashtray.

Mornings, and fluttering curtains
luminous with a new day's compulsions;
coughing of waterpipes through walls, quick gushes
of radio-music, frying from cramped kitchenettes –
the whole house permeable, like limestone or gorgonzola.

But when from outside I looked up,
the blank pane glinting above a tree
gave nothing away. "You'd never guess who lived there,"
I said to my workday self. Nor the girls
in the office, with twinsets, hairdos and boyfriends,
lives fitted to rings, and leaving to have children.
Only at nightfall I lugged back,
past plateglass windows where like heraldry
paired diners faced across starched cloths,
and furtively in, and up, my leaking hoard,
careful not to knock the landing-table
where pot-plants browned, past doors, and shut my door.

And spread it out. Digested some into
the novel I was writing – she who, tracked
since a catching of eyes in a corridor
richened into romantic definition,
talked to at last, had bored me: "Jane's face
sustained beneath her fringe a permanent lift
of slight surprise." "Which settles her" – now on
to the journal that then seemed worth keeping –
"Besides, I could never have afforded to take her out."
And washed the whole lot down with gas-ring coffee.

Those were the days: all I owned going into one suitcase,
everything possible, everything serving my turn;
when being a loner flukily squared
with what's less put up with, being alone,
in the darkness, at one with the slow
breathing of suburbs like lyrics expanding in stanzas.

North Derry Nocturne

I

An unapologetic
Irish sky decays:
sunset, and Donegal's
ridge lies out on water

crimson-rimmed, small clouds
like fluffs of ink above
on orange fading to blue.
I watch the embers burn

out. Now only far
Greencastle's twinkle, where
boats nose from the land's shadow
to harvest a salt darkness.

II

I load the Bendix – round
and round all goes in the wash –
and walk down Prospect Road
to raise my glass in the Anchor:

the old familiar faces,
the University matters.
These horses of instruction!
Where are the wiser tigers

of wrath? Outside and headed
this way last evening, a car
blew up: they found an arm
tattooed "for God and Ulster".

III

We talk our last pints through;
your man here, blond, flush-faced,

degree in Greek and Latin,
grew up inside all this:

"But those were quieter days.
The big house was still owned
by mad aristocrats –
the goings-on up there,

locking each other in cupboards,
disowning heirs! I'd go
for chestnuts to the estate.
They chased me waving shotguns."

IV

Now the gun's outside
the plantation wall, and trigger
pulled. The headlights catch
only a moving swathe

of scrubby verge, with bracken
smashed, and one dead hedgehog.
We pass the Bush round, sip
its thread of warmth. Unseen

the billowing hills pegged down
by stony farms attuned
to ancient disciplines,
bringing to growth, to market.

V

"My uncle's a country man,"
says one. "He's not been known
to construct an entire sentence.
But he could keep a farm.

He knew of just one way
with vermin: take the gun.

And so he'd keep the country.
But he couldn't hold his son.

Des married a go-go dancer
from Strabane, a Teague.
They've two wains now, in England."
All's black outside the car.

VI

As last month in the Tube
before I came from England,
I watched straphanging faces
assuming some next station

and thought, What if we stopped
for ever in this tunnel,
or, not rising out
at Finchley Road, the train

dipped, and whooshed straight through?
So – we read the papers,
plan lectures, double-glazing;
now, coffee-time again.

VII

Dropped back from which, indoors
I leave the curtains open:
set desk, the anglepoise's
glow, ringed mug, and dimmed

bookshelves – thus to cruise
night, the town's few roofs
heaving vague, subsumed
to the Atlantic groundswell;

precise in focused light
ink's strict notation charts

the spinning nebulae,
the labyrinthine self.

VIII

Where the Minotaur of soul
bellows darkly, ramps
mazed in intricacies,
gorges pale ideals.

All, killer in the night,
the poets, demagogues,
take as they find for world,
apotheosise these

confines. But mine those walls
with imagination's fuse –
poor souls in a rough field
adrift in stars and sea.

IX

And I, returned, who hang
these blanched sheets to the moon,
feet tangling in wet grass?
I think three weeks back to

that girl in the Penge Chinese:
"They send you anywhere,
I see it all, meet friends.
But you know how it is.

It's like you're in the dark,
and strike match after match.
I could chuck the agency
I know . . . But it's not that . . ."

X

And so, I wait for dawn's
pure green and silver, sea
calmed by soft arms of coast;
Portstewart clarifying

around me, white and frail
as shells these houses clasped
to rock, so rootless might
be gone with the next tide;

as when, in skins, men first
leant upon spears to see
dream-clear Donegal
sunlit across the water.

From the Other Country

But you do not consider how long I have lived in this country.
Its skies move through my skull, and the changing light
over the water; like whales the humped mountains
surface in my dreams, and never were trees
thwart like these in flight from the salt harsh gales.

The customs of the people, it is true,
are not mine; in farms and one-street towns
they enact strict rituals of thrift, worship, pleasure.
Lights burn late where slow accounts are reckoned,
the drunk crashes prone in dying embers,

and beneath tribal tokens, ancient recitations.
Often indeed through main street and glen
drums throb savage annunciation, the door
opens to a rain of bullets, car-lights pick out
the corpse in a ditch. "It's a madness going on,"

they say. Did you think madness so dull?
Look: how finite among the weltering green
these settlements, no margins to nourish the odd.
Knowing their place, they grow, pray, wed, kill, die.
Even their knowing smiles have a terrible innocence

which you do not understand. Nor, though you hear,
how their soft gutturals and singing intonation
infect my accent. I am welcomed
in bars and corner-shops, with "It's a soft night."
And yes, I have loved their girls.

See, where fine white clouds drift high above the meadow
the small farm daydreams all doors open:
they are all gone round the bend of the field, out of change.
Behind the clock on the mantel dust thickens on letters
strangely-deciphered, from children "across the water".

From where, too, on my screen come shimmering
images of the old labyrinthine cities,
sanities. Which I can revisit, resume
undetected; noticing how they find
bestial or glamorous our banalities,

and do not see the detail beneath stark outlines.
I am no longer sure that I wish to return,
even though it is winter here now, the sky and land
seeping greyly together. Unsettled, defined
by difference, I find I can live with this,

am strangely involved in, call it, a climate.
Yes, as the mad wind rises, sets the sea
resonating, whips waves white, and plucks
tiles from thin roofs, above which gulls
weave lamentation's dissonant vocables.

The Mountains

I do not talk of daytime, when one can choose;
though whether, already exhausted, to follow what shrugs
beyond the horizon, knowing it always will,
or turn back, either feels like failure,
and the brooks raising noise like something wanting answer.
But it is the nights, when the mountains choose me,
bare, humped, unscalable, that prove possession.
I have seen a face against that backcloth
eyes pouring intensity, the streets between
minutely familiar, mapped with memories
like lilac-scents, some turnings now forbidden,
and houses to be called at or no more
allowed. These things deflected my purpose,
and the air filled with the voices of the girls
I had been young with calling in their children;
still hauntingly that clear brow beyond me.
The mountains are my sleep's wild hinterland,
they shift, usurp known territories. Once,
above roofs at the edge of a town a stile,
and path leading up the climbing eye; there were people
ascending, returning; some strayed to rest in the sunlight.
But down in the street they denied the stile,
and the slopes shut off, cloud spilling down ravines.
It was last night I hit the summit.
My glider had found a thermal current, and rising
rode it. . . After the smash I looked from a ledge
upon greenness strewn with white cottages by their turfstacks
and slate-dark lakes, all intricately rimmed
with yellow strand; far out to sea
stood Rathlin, Aran, the Blaskets; and I held
the whole world's curve, revolved it slowly. . .
Then came down; the man whose slant along
the upper slopes I crossed was real enough,
on Brandon once, he'd leant, told how all weathers
took him high as his sheep, and for no peak's sake.
Whin and heather tore my clothes, I filled

a shoe with peaty water, found the road,
at last crashed bleeding through swing doors. No head
looked up. They said, "There are no mountains."

Reading Habit

At the end of each chapter, the end of the novel,
some of the characters are always left talking;
they drift out on a blank leaf,
paired or alone, down indeterminate vistas.

I put down the book. Leaves cry out
on autumnal boughs, are scythed by the driving wind helplessly,
the sky ebbs violet over the rooftops.
It is the close of another day,

and the lights that spring on show some characters still left talking,
framed in their windows a dinner party, a girl
brushing her hair, grey screens flickering
news of death picking off others, elsewhere.

So with "good-nights" at doorsteps and bus-stops,
assuring "until tomorrow", "take care",
we float wrapped in coloured dreams out on a pure
white sheet, its comforting blankness.

Those who are no longer with us, the tyrant
cut down in an early chapter, the drowned fiancé,
the aunt who fought cancer meanly, must have been different,
there not for themselves, but for us to react to.

Not in my book, one saying
"He, by what he did, and left undone,
and how, and why, helps us shape our perspectives" –
the untrodden page still realisable before him.

In Highgate Wood

A flicker of sun through leaves in Highgate Wood,
this moment of recognition: I who know
no kin find myself open intently
in a willed, almost religious relinquishing,

as if to diffuse among this ceaseless play
some latent thing so near in me it asks
to be named all that I now forego
as what it might have been: I say, "My son."

Whispering translucencies take up the merely
personal into their green going-on
ageing within each season's restlessness.
Another spring. I lean against

a hornbeam's fluted trunk to follow up
the frail slant of a silver birch bole hung
with tatters of bark like peeling paint.
Slow bramble smothers cut lengths of felled tree,

and the bones of a dumped pram are patiently
digested. Always the forest, underfoot
its dead green softening to renew; and nothing
I can bestow: this is, as from a child,

a receiving. See how delicately wrought
that cherry-tree declares its blossoming,
drifts of flowers like conjurings from snow
almost, so pure and candid:

luminous thing, it tricks the eye
to seem itself condensation of mere air
floating it, yet is earthed in darkness.
Brief one of many, time unique as flesh.

Playing Through Old Games of Chess

A crane-fly trembles in the windowpane
as it has since before there were windows . . .
I play through old games of chess: their rich diapason
a blossoming in the room, as of huge heavy-headed roses.

Outside, the hottest summer since records began,
and the traffic-lights signalling insane morse,
a jabber of red green amber, somewhere a computer
has overheated, fouling the traffic and tempers

are overheated, and all along the Thames
the bridges shove themselves over from metal expansion.
Ah, the ecologists say, it is carbon dioxide
irreversibly building up in the upper atmosphere

due to industrial waste, and all kinds of waste
accumulate irreversibly, and we record it,
even the mineral ores of language processed through
to a standing slag beyond recycling;

and economists say it is the economy overheated.
The plane trees shimmer through rising petrol fumes,
and children's voices ascend to tinkle against the bowl
of a blue sky hazed with entropy, our last heat-death.

I reset the pieces and start again:
Steinitz versus Tchigorin, Ruy Lopez, Morphy Defence,
Havana, 1892, and decorously
the opposite knights step forth, the kings are castled to safety

for a while. And still for a while
beyond the cities in meadows (but a hum of traffic hanging)
the cows, as then, stand four-square over their shadows,
while one by one white petals slip into sun-dappled water

to float, for a while; and the woods are dark with summer,
greenness sloping to greenness to a far

horizon marked with the faint stroke of a steeple
as it has been since before there were

– steeples, I almost said. At least as when
all history seemed a sort of sunlit incline upwards,
with problems like the Balkans, abolishing cholera, crime,
certainly soluble, and change meant improvement,

hygiene, gas cooking, fast travel, the bioscope.
Beneath "Truman, Hanbury, Buxton & Comps. Entire"
the old photograph shows clay pipes and boaters around an ale-bench,
and Spoonbeam is not out at lunch for Lancs for ever,

while at dusk, his cycle-lamp catching gold motes
along deep lanes where roots twist and convolvulus clings,
comes Cholmondeley to talk, over whiskey by leaded windows,
of *The Origin of Species* or *The Idylls of the King*.

The pawn-structure looks sound, across the board *andante*
the full orchestration unfolds, with recurring motifs and grace-notes,
rounding Good Hope the *Ariel* bringing home tea from China,
cablegrams under the sea, while in Afghan hill-posts

or where a delta's archipelagos of bamboo huts
coalesce to a port of old palaces, crumbling pagodas,
men with iron moustaches bat out their time
outstaring all sundowns from the verandah.

Of course, through the looking-glass all was different,
and moving forward got you nowhere, the miners
stonily piling their barrows after the latest eviction
cannot see their great-grandsons' Cortinas, package-tour fritterings,

and the husband who tendered with flowers the most honourable intentions
is hanging his stovepipe hat on the bedposts of whores;

and every life dark-edged, the hushed death-rooms, the infant
graves,
and perhaps it is all the tinman's dream

who stationed at the street corner pedals his grinding-wheel
for ever. And as for the countless hordes
of Indians and Chinese, it is not their game
at all, they have nothing to learn but patience.

Exchange of queens: the general liquidation
which follows seems to favour white, a sacrificial
manoeuvre clinches things, for a while. If today
in Flanders the farmer again wades through barley where all nature

was murdered, still the old dynasts have toppled like chess-kings,
and however we go through the motions again
(the squares are being done up, houses wormy with their past
are scoured, the cellars blocked off as if there were bones down
in them,

layers of cheap flowered paper torn from each wall),
or trace the lines not followed, unrealised combinations
in notes as much as the moves played part of the game,
the quality of that long, lost summer cannot be restored

– when June rang like a gong for Pax Britannica,
and Europe's chordage held the world enthralled;
and in London, St. Petersburg, Vienna or Baden Baden
the old chess-masters' arias thrilled. Until Lasker, who

would research Relativity, talk with Einstein, flee
the Nazis, shifted a piece irrevocably changing
the chemistry of the game, its lovely architectonics;
while a crane-fly trembled in the windowpane.

That Pass in the Night

A hush of fine rain,
upon deepening lawns
each house drifts back, settling
round T.V.'s wan glow.

Then clear over all
the streets' loose ends and aimless
wires, lights, I see
a ship in the bay.

Or where should be the bay:
the headlands have vanished,
no sea, nor horizon,
just an indigo-grey

solution, that black
lozenge suspended,
red port light and rich
gold suffusing the stern.

Enviable far world!
close under dim steam-pipes
hot soup, jokes, card-playing
– now perhaps looking back

through a finger-rubbed port-hole
on this shore's lit filament
afloat upon fathomless
space, as to home.

Tomorrow will bring back
bold street-fronts, curved headlands,
sea clear: the ship gone,
or our world rolled on.

Stepping Westward, Donegal

"And stepping westward seemed to be
A kind of *heavenly* destiny."
Wordsworth

At times I could believe I'd even reached . . .
But the land shrugged on and west, and west again,
through Creeslough the hedged pasture giving way
to drystone walls, a frail net cast

over what heaved savage now, huge boulders standing
intact like eggs, and the sentinel long hump
of Muckish rising. Then the other side
where the gap road wound close under the mountain.

In slow processional cloud-shadows ascended
a calm flank filigreed with scree, and water
somewhere ravelling hoarsely; the climb
unfolded vistas bluing to far ranges.

And from Calabber through the afternoon
lines of turfcutters bent to a brackish landscape
as like a further planet Errigal
reared its serene cone. A turn looked down

on a lough spread in the rift: intensely green
those deeper fields; some dwellings, planted beechwood
smudging the shadow of an old estate
beneath the frozen surge of the Poisoned Glen.

So to descend, and find the church roofless, lapped
with thick grass starry with milkwort, speedwell, vetch,
and pedestalled on the little stone bridge
old stumps of statues long since knocked away,

but bees weighting wild rhododendron and
the bank tumbling its primroses down to a stream

that sustained between alders one flickering dance of sunlight,
seemed to reach some meant core of the day.

– But was not all. One last extremity:
green, violet, glittering white that strand's heaped stones,
and no more to do with man than the unnameable
light on sea ringing to lost horizons.

That carried along the whole return, with travelling
lines of mountains, past the turfcutters crouched
still over antique spades, red weathered faces
lifting incuriously after the car,

till Muckish sank behind like a slow whale,
telling nothing. Brought back, just this one
crystalline pure ellipsoid, paperweight
here heavy with all it holds unbroken.

Pictures from Donegal

for Vic Willi

Through Rathmelton then
six miles of turns and lanes,
"Ask for Greer's cottage"

– in the heart of silence
and greenery dripping fuchsia.
We'd sit outside all day

sunburning, the chessboard
aligned so you could manage
all moves but knight-leaps,

and talked, of everything –
your transatlantic voice
a buzz-saw in the pure air –

but most, of what you'd come
here to, sick Ireland
and its maddest flourishes:

"Some Provies dressed as nuns
robbed a Coleraine bank,
were lifted drinking in Garvagh . . ."

"I used to have," you said,
"a laugh like yours before
my chest-muscles went."

Vic, I envy your
clear sight: from your wheelchair
gazing across the Swilly

to pick out where light gleamed
on Inishowen far
fields cut since yesterday.

I had learned to empty
your drainage-bag, hook
the cup to your withering hand,

had come, having the time,
to be "of use", and surely
wasn't much. We loafed

till the girls drove back from Derry.
– Which you'd seen also, bombed
to bits, the soldiers,

and an old dear yammering
"When yous go back, just tell them
we're not all monsters."

Then every evening out
around mountains and valleys
firing your camera at

glittering heather, turfstacks,
sunset over more bays
than you'd ever remember

– remember the seals off Fanad,
with Donegal flinging
wild arms to the Atlantic?

It needs a place far gone
as this for me to realise
our science-fiction age:

"Yes, probably the bomb
will drop," I think
for the first time in years,

while you are staring at
intricate drystone walls
netting tiny holdings

on an empty headland. Yes,
people have starved here,
been driven away;

this cottage, where returning
to fumble with tilley-lamps
and well-water is for us

a week going primitive,
for two hundred years
cocooned remote lives

that never saw towns,
our electric civilisation
a car-ride away

– yet were near as first light
woke me. You too perhaps
(as well as the tang of guinness

and "Is it an Anglo-Canadian
consortium yous are,
these your secretaries from Derry?")

have taken back what camera
and eyesight are blank to:
beneath the flowered wallpaper

old scuffmarks, burns, an odour
outlasting us and all
on our chirruping radio.

Encounter

And now the party is over. Level our heads
above burnt matches, wine-stains; our discarded
whiskey-glasses spread, a paradigm
of what each has told, the retrospective map
of disarray; and intermingled now
our points of bearing, gleaming remnants nag
for sleight of reflection, kaleidoscopic pattern.

When raising of blinds lets brutal daylight in
on wider ravage, tinfoil scorched and scarred,
food mashed on paper plates, ash, scatterings
of glass, I say, "We know where we are."
We can manage our clearing. Through to this terrain
strange under our feet, that asks no name, is not
to be betrayed. Now try my eyes again.

On the Mend

"And what if the patient, whose sores you are washing, does not at once show how grateful he is to you, but, on the contrary, begins to torment you with his whims, without noticing or valuing your kindly services? What if he should start shouting at you, demanding something from you rudely (as often happens when people are in great pain) – what then? Will you still go on loving him?"

The Brothers Karamazov

So now you are on the mend. Upon the lawn
outside the Female Ward we lounge, eat squares
of chocolate, and drink apple-juice; like stars
the weave of speedwells blue in springy grass.

It was not thus when we first visited.
The ambulance that had brought you from your last
bitching, sleepless, frantic, then mad week
outside, you called "the Celestial Insomnibus",

your mind raced manic, spinning wheels with no
purchase on the real; unsteadily
you craved to see life whole: "Bring me a globe
I'll reconcile Marx and Christianity"

(in tantrums at a world that would not see),
"I'd turn it upside-down and find my twin
in the Antipodes." So David said
"Take that lawn as the globe's top bit, start there."

The door between was locked then. "But I'll shrink
until I go through the keyhole," you explained.
Meanwhile, confined to nightwear, scribbled reams . . .
The doctors said: "Her judgement's very poor."

We soft-shoe-shuffled down a corridor,
noting your institutional drugged pace.

And, on the wall, a fire-alarm beside
which the standard printed notice read

"IN CASE OF FIRE", then every usual clause,
"1. Break glass" etc. . . Some loony had
crossed these through, in staggering capitals
substituted just, "I'D PUT IT OUT."

– Regardless of ferocity, extent?
Infantile omnipotence! the new
problem-solving technique for all! IN CASE
OF BEING SICK – GET WELL. IN CASE OF LOVE . . .

"Wouldn't it be nice if we could fall in love,
marry, have children," confided your friend Anne
childishly. But, "David frightens me,
like Dr Who," at first. Your polar twin,

schizoid, depressive, Anne talked of her "fears",
when she talked. But mostly hunched in trance
gazed into no-space; roamed in odd forays
as we tippled the hospital-canteen lucozade.

Then once, while fingersnapping patients lurched
failing to dance (others impassive stared)
to T.V.'s "Top of the Pops", Anne deadpan told
how, this time, it had happened she came here:

"I was going to hit my mother with a saw.
She was sawing. So I took the saw
to hit her. So my sister got me here.
My sister's right. They make me well in here."

Anne's fears, your hypomanic ferment of
ideas, aggressions, such are impulses
we all know. "Health" is pragmatic, it appears:
can the world cope with one, or one with it?

"It's chemical," they say. When you snapped back
at my mild "no" to your "All growing-up
is coming to terms with one's father," since my tone
"recalled" him, She needs help, I thought, self-curbed.

Well: you "got your clothes" (the idiom here
and emblem of recovering); and then
your room's french-window was unlocked, so we
and others visiting walked you on the lawn.

And Anne, as if a switch had dropped, clicked back
to "normal", talkative, interested, live;
and has her clothes. So now for the last time
before your coming-out the four of us

sit on this grass, your sunlit room behind
decked with flowers, cards, its pastel shades
a cool interior; all here you know best
are on the mend. It's garden-partyish.

Except, of course, that others are brought in
each day. "That beautiful girl," you said, found drunk,
fouled and pregnant in a Derry street;
the youth who'd blown up an ice-cream van, for

"the ultimate onanistic thrill," you joke.
And also in the Male Ward, there's our friend
the alcoholic poet. Visiting
you he scatters litter, yanks a door

to wrench a lucozade-top off so gouts
splatter annoying the cleaners. Insufferable
the suffering can be: by turns he fawns,
insults, all nerve-ends frayed; once, turkey-faced

accused we'd swayed his nerve-worn estranged wife,
then waddled huffing down the corridor.
Well, outside, in a Belfast pub they'd smash
his face for less. "But he needs help," we say.

So, the bell rings calling you for lunch,
quietly to accept your "medication" where
three weeks ago they'd hold you down, inject,
as you curled screaming distant in lost time.

Outside will care for you. But may not care
to be always pleasanter to you than you
to it which falls back on no such "needs help"
exoneration. Judgement that is poor

will be called bad, not "illness": morally
health entails responsibility where
infantilism never put fires out.
Meanwhile, for outside, you've fresh-waved your hair.

The Interviews

for Elizabeth Sheldon

Ledged high in glass and steel, the Committee Room:
"So why do you want to be . . .?" That is, to join us.
From ten stock replies, you select for your mood,
think to yourself "Choose a number, try for the jackpot;"
while your gaze skids out to that dying orange cloud-rent.

Or they are "unsure of the lines of your career,"
"Of course, it's a battlefield here," or "The crucial art
is delegation" – and can you think of one reason
why anyone's right for this except (which you are)
the sort who on principle would refuse it?

Often, they like you, you seem "creative",
though "here we've developed a team-philosophy."
You are interviewed longer than anyone else, and given
a second tea; but the post is given
to that dud in a deep-pile suit, or the mouse from Garstang.

Long after the cleaners have crunched up the debris, leaving
these rooms in a mist of purifying aerosol,
in the icy misshapen hours when you cannot sleep,
or delegate not sleeping, and facing the final
questions finds no reason for anything ever,

you take all night to the high lines of the moors;
there are forests with silence folded under their leaves;
and every motor-way mile phones on posts skid past
your hurtling box, each *Why do you want to be?*
foundering in your wake's black wastes unfurling.

Accounts Payable

Sunlight striking from an angle upon wet slates
seizes from daily rails the minds behind
the faces behind newspapers, floating them
high above blackened girders, stained brick arches,
factories frail as cartons, sweeps of roofline like
the patterns left in sand when the tide ebbs,
to that if-only space where all might turn . . .
Until, the terminus's dark lid sliding
over, trains draw in; lives reassume their frames.

"That's Mr Sims's office. He's in charge.
But off this week having all his teeth out.
So meanwhile we've got Eric. He's all right.
When he's all right. Here's what we do in here,
we match these delivery-notes with invoices,
checking the quantities, we mustn't pay
for more than what we get. So query all
discrepancies. Mr Anderson will start you,
he's been here in Accounts Payable forty years."

These hands, crawling between ruled margins,
so many faces clenched against something like fists.
"My friend Doris said, she said when she
was a nurse she fed a patient custard who'd
died. Well he could only take slops and
just lying there you'd hardly tell, she said,
I mean she'd spooned it in for ages,
but he'd passed on in the night. Gave her a turn.
I'd rather be a telephonist than that."

But Maureen is wondering whether Eric
really is fucking June the Comptometer operator,
and can you tell from the look of them now standing there?
No flies on Eric: "Fancies himself. Still, rather
him than that old Anderson stuck here
a century and all he knows or cares about
is writing copperplate. Them times have gone,
'You been dead you old fool for years' I said to him,
only I didn't. His legs, all blotched with bloodclots."

So, lunchtimes stroll about past flyblown shops,
hotels, that kiosk where oranges glow;
note the chiropodist's window cluttered with plaster casts
of feet deformed or maimed; at junctions meet
beneath plucked brows the distilled gaze
risen from multitudinous spoiled beds
(and how much pain can one head hold?);
or in the museum stare at the mummified princess,
lids shrivelled, which four thousand years ago . . .

While, between the sweet and the bill,
"It's easier anyway to say yes than no,
they're mostly married of course, but that means nothing
these days. Friends? Oh, friends are all right. I've friends,
I'm not the type to be much on my own.
But you, you're deep, so you know what I mean,
it's someone to really talk to. And there's more to sex
than just sex. The agency send you anywhere.
I could chuck the agency, but it's not that . . ."

And the aeroplanes are catapulted over and over
all afternoon, and gently in stained hands
Mr Anderson lifts his tea-mug, half
hearing Mrs Wilkes ("I told my Jan
when baby's sick you don't wanna give it milk,
milk lies on its chest, milk's thickening . . ."),
and thinking how all is different now. It isn't:
as always the old pity the young
freedom that leaves nothing to betray,

while they are pitied struggle that has left nothing.
And both are right, and wrong; and discrepancies are queried,
until the hour when starlings descend twittering
on ashen roofs, and the sky is delicately mauve,
and ghosted reflections harden on the pane:
Shall I go out? Or not go out? Not liking
either these days. Nor what my head holds . . .
"Until tomorrow," "Take care," "Don't do what I'd not," . . .
And indeed one might as well say yes as no.

And yes, says the city, stripteasing in neon,
setting heads spinning, perfumed, expensive to enjoy;
it whispers from doorways, trickles in music from gratings;
and the young, who pay her to tell them lies, or lonely
wipe their tears away on her dirtiest corners,
fresh faces from the branches of childhoods
rooted in small parks and suburbs, shove through
knowing as broken those they push past; not knowing
that this is their turning-point, and it is gone.

"Follow the coloured lights", says the Underground . . .
But this is another tunnel, and longer and darker,
still tilting down, the carriage-lights wan,
and many who used to be in the compartment are gone,
and anyway everyone really journeys alone
to discrepant destinations; and what lies thickening
on the chest is not milk . . . "I saw his teeth drop.
By when they took him out his face was blue.
Old. Anderson. Well, his account is settled."

But there is no reason why the train
should ever stop; or start. Or as someone is saying
anywhere (the lights may be dim; or strobe-lights),
"It's like those airport carousels, round and round
and you panic thinking that what belongs to you
will never be delivered." And someone else:
"I once took flying-lessons. Compared with a car
so free, no keeping in lanes, or not doing U-turns
whenever you feel like. You pay through the nose for it . . ."

Yet after the traffic dims, the last door
slams, a pause, when the imagination listens:
to the maimed pulse of the suburbs troubling the darkness
the furniture settling ton by ton into fitted carpets;
from beds a dissonant music of wild dreams rising.
Framed at a sill, a man lets night in,
not so to understand that whorl of stars,
but rather as if hoping they might him.
Dropped newsprint blows to rags down moonlit rails.

from "*Given Worlds*"

3. *War Memoir*

"Jim went down with the *Hood*" brings back
my war: carried beneath cold stars
to earthy shelter. Those bangs? "Just
night-time noises buses make dear."

Before-the-war, all sweets and fruit,
an Eden missed by being born
in its refugee-camp. Which transferred
me in 'forty-four to a farm:

one windmill locking sky on land,
Eyetie prisoners, Nellie the horse;
the barn where I touched tongues with June.
And as I grasped the universe was

War, again the city's skein
of trolleybus-wires spread overhead,
strange "Peace" declared; leaving for years
my playgrounds, bomb-sites, pillbox, tank-traps.

4. *Suburban Eden*

White shirtsleeves pumped the August dusk,
chasing a ball. In winter mists'
silence, only black boughs dripping,
it seemed like miles from any house.

So, in the park, for years we grew;
sprawled balancing the sun upon
nonchalantly-raised knee; there came
girls, to wake new pains; yet still

within a world sealed by the sky's
rim; that never was aware

until too late, and shaken from
its branches we felt city stone.

And one cannot return, except
to look: shrunk, all's still going on;
girls call, the ball rolls loose; my foot
holds back. One kick might shatter glass.

5. *Downhill all the Way*

Ten-thirty. Dave, their Progress Chaser,
gasps "It's stifling, someone please
open a window." When you do
soot sifts in, specks cuffs and files.

Eleven. And a butterfly:
Dawn and June bat it with carbons,
shrieking. Ron stamps dockets, frowns
intent on 1960 when

he'll sit where Wilderspin now sits
in the swivel chair, Costs Manager,
Ascough, Stiffkey & Co. . . But looks
shrunk, like something xeroxed half-size.

And as the minute-hand limps past noon
(the butterfly is limp between two panes)
Dave says, as this time every day,
"Downhill all the way now." It is.

6. *Way Back*

Clearing after a party or
another lover come and gone,
before the Tube and the next cup
there swims into her levelled head's

conjugated retrospects,
as her eyes admit fresh snow
giving urban sunrise back,
that winter twenty years ago:

"In twenty years we will come back"
they kissed. She could go now alone,
see emptied husks upon such white:
mill, village, church, and youth. Composed,

unsuccouring. Suffering no loss.
Each spring rinsed millstone moors blank green,
fresh water fills the valley's throat,
black chimneys faintly suppurate.

10. *Cast Up*

Cast up on lawns in wicker chairs
the old wait for the sun to drop,
hump-shouldered, facing screens of trees,
hands fiddling with their knitting, book.

What should we say to them? That we
have also been far out, in rain,
in passion? Patiently they turn
countenances rubbed, effaced,

or scored deep by more tides than they
remember, tokens of enough
weather; not distracted from
gold charring at the garden's end.

Outgrowths of themselves they seem,
hobbling in, from habit propped
on shapes long warped from, taller once
in hailstorms, distant lanes' white heat.

11. *Then*

Finger's up which ink has crept
entwined in grass, grasshoppers' hum,
stipple of leaves above, somewhere
a woodpigeon. So, having come

past raw brick at the town-end, down
the banked convolvulus-hung lane
where girls bowl hoops and white dust scuffs,
he lies suspended on this verge,

flutterings of that fritillary and
a spider eating something winged
incised for ever on his brain,
July's indifferent green lid

drowsing. Tonight, sprat supper, dad
talking of Asquith, Bosnia.
A passing carter sculpts deep ruts,
calls out "Daresay it will hold up."

14. *Bunhill Fields*

Crammed, blackening, subsiding, warped,
some weathered past deciphering,
dissenters' gravestones; railed off from
what's smoothed to lawn and flowerbeds,

where pensioners put out to grass
and girls with limpid eyes and prams
sun through the weekday afternoon,
as Milton, blind nearby, once did.

The risen City overlooks
here Cromwells, Wesleys, and the bones
of Bunyan, Blake, Defoe. Above
and underneath the grass now, stillness.

Broken by what taps my cheek
flaked from the opulence of trees
repeating autumn's fall of life
to headstone, greensward, marking time.

Retirement

At ease with a glass of wine,
sunset pearling the sky above
Shropshire hills, blackberries
ripening in the hedges.

Gaius Mannius Secundus
of the tribe Pollia, 31 years
in the Tungrian regiments, after
the fighting in North Britain

having discharge, citizenship,
settling for this:
Viroconium's paved thoroughfares,
forum, and public baths;

secure from the murderous rites
in the uncivil mountains westward,
not to speak of the wheeling
hordes of the German forests;

as for fabulous Rome,
its poisonings, coups, executions,
(other veterans have seen it)
– better this peaceable periphery

where the writ of the Emperor
Caesar Trajanus Hadrianus
Augustus, son of the deified
Trajanus, and such mumbo-jumbo,

is pared of insanities
to a network orderly as these roads,
bureaucratic routines
enjoyed by the Romanised Celts.

Fluorescent lights reflect
from glass over unearthed denarii,

a holed kettle, Samian ware;
a model-reconstruction of

that place then never knowing
England due to go over it
like a tidal wave, a succession:
the blood-edged Saxon darkness

slowly civilising to churches;
more fighting, fortifications;
blackberries ever ripening
through a land's long cultivation.

Beyond the museum's windows
Shrewsbury's traffic snarls;
and "Timberland" the Home Improvers,
Credit Facilities.

On Mannius's tombstone
still crisp Latin; lions and pinecone
are sculpted symbols of afterlife:
reclining, wherever, beneath us.

Death in the Family

i.m. Leonard Waterman, 1900-1979

"I have to tell you that your father died,
suddenly, a heart-attack, last week."

Who am I weeping for? Mother,
is it the first time of your own accord
you've mentioned him in thirty years?
You write: "It was a comfort knowing him
there somewhere. It's my young life cut away."

"Father. My father," has the distant flavour
of childhood's licorice, convolvulus
along the lane to Highams Park where he,
bespectacled, in brown, rowed us on water.

And you "could never talk of it" until
five years ago: it seemed he'd kept away
reluctantly; sent money; was in the Shropshire phone-book.
My sister dialled, heard far burring, then
put down the phone. Nor fearfully
did I track to that door. Now never can.

Paths closed, for you, me, that vestigial man.

Yet all once cherishing stays somewhere true:
you both aged my age now adopting me;
and, dapple of light or time disfiguring
his face, those careworn clerk's hands still upon
the oars, on summer's trembling lake.

A History of Ideas

When I was eighteen I took up a blank white sheet
and heading it CREDO wrote out the lot,
needing to know what I thought, and especially why
no God exists: nobler so, if a pity.

At thirty, notes jotted while travelling, on margins
and envelope-backs: some shimmered to poems
nagging fragmentarily at why so much seemed
a pity, not noble, no God now in question.

Near forty, dark with my words, I helplessly dream
heaven where all that's been broken moves healed
as in dance: blue jug on its shelf; summer walks we intended.
Wake knowing ignobly such hunger self-pity.

The Ould Boy

Cold as ice. He'd never notice you
when you four were all wains. Left all of that
up to your ma. Just came in and went out.
Friends? He'd boozing mates, no real friends
you'd say. Asked "What's he really like?" say "Hands.
They're his gift. He could do anything."
In wood. Or stone. "That picture in the hall,
no educated taste, but details perfect."
And never trained. Did nothing with it. "Just
a housepainter, when what he should have been's
a craftsman as few can be, say restoring
rood-screens for old churches wrecked with dry rot."
What reared him offered swagger, drums, King Billy.
"The Ould Boy's maybe kicked his life away
not knowing his way out from under it.
Modelled himself instead on Cary Grant,
even curling his lip like this when talking."
"He'd come home stocious late on Christmas Eve,
no food or heat in the house, and never caring."
Yet made that garden shed, slats firm, all wired
for electricity; those amazing toys:
"The jack-in-the-box, it's in the attic now,
pops up like *this*. He made the spring, the box,
from scratch, and it'll last two hundred years."
"You felt he'd done it for himself, not you.
Yet really he's done nothing for himself."
Twelve years back, when your mother hurled one more
burnt supper out, he packed and went. And showed
no interest since. You'll see him now, round bars,
hair still that black there's a blue sheen off it.
"He'll reach you ten pounds now, it's sad as if
he's lonely, but who'd know what's in his head?"
"He used to read. Read poetry. Aloud.
Fitzgerald's *Rubáiyát*. The only times
I mind that I felt close. His voice so, slowing:
'What! . . . did the Hond, then . . . of the Potther . . . *she-ak*?'"

For Her Thirty-Fifth Birthday

Becalmed, one almost might have thought,
after your havocked years, now lodged
by the grey church upon the hill.
Wide windows gaze on shrugging green.

Only a wobble in your tone
as you try calculating things:
"Alone's all right. Then with my son
I'm not alone. Also there is . . ."

I've listened. "It's clandestine, but
really is love. He's sensitive,
hurt if I've gone out when he phones."
Which troubles you you tell the wife

"he'll never leave". I know. She knows.
She rings you when he's home depressed.
His prints hang here, but not your gifts
on him. So, "all" you "ask from life".

Life grins across the room, or yawns.
Whistling its own tunes. Up to much
beyond you. Out to live it up
carelessly may run down folk

at crossroads for the hell of it;
gossips; plots strange gatherings;
drunkenly gropes you; knows no tact.
There for the taking. Not put out.

Today, snow where I wake evokes
your pallor hesitating back
from spacious pane to desk or stove.
Pure thaw-drops bead; do not yet drop.

from *"Out for the Elements"*

Starry tonight, and repetitious
sea harassing the empty strand,
as when it first cast adventitious
staggering life upon the land;
through sleights of wondrous generation
since to attain a consummation
in filaments of light I see
stacked on the Prom: humanity
with all its complex apparatus,
deep-freezers, televisions, cars,
banks, supermarkets, churches, bars,
shows what once kindled to create us
subtilised now to a weird grace-
note shimmering on time and space.

The sand beneath my feet caressing
negligently each emptied shell,
dropped cans and condoms, spreads expressing
only conclusive flatness. Well
clear of its first-and-last mnemonic
and breakers issuing their sonic
premonitions, mankind who feigns
whole worlds dreamed to exalted planes,
within those intricate wired boxes
saying things like "computer sales",
"topspin forehand", "don't tell tales",
"I'm not contracepting" foxes
comprehension with monkey-tricks:
arts, avocations, politics.

Marvellous are the anthills, skuas,
acacias, zebras, whales, yet none
gone so tortuously askew as
man so inventively has done
from first imperatives. How did it
come about? How could nature bid it
we should attain such livings as

insurance, market-research, and jazz,
mining for coal, or crawling under
purring metal contraptions, or
inspecting wickets, or the law?
It all bends the mind; and no wonder
that some are put away, convinced
they're parrots or the Queen, brains minced.

Small babies born to suck, laugh, cry on
their mothers' breasts, pure animal,
grow to learn how to tie a tie on,
and say "Don't get emotional,"
budgeting life away, its flicker
never possessed streams ever quicker:
first toy, first fuck, child, grandchild, stroke,
then that's your lot. I could invoke
anthologies of the grim ending,
mad, murdered, maimed, mocked, crucified
by surgical art. Most just subside
slowly though into what's past mending,
shopping around until they're gone,
unmissed where fleets of prams roll on.

Or take that teashop in South Norwood
where I once grew up, named "The Horst
Café": every year more and more would
alter it with paint to read "Worst
Café", and the man and his wife who
owned the place change it back, a life you
could hardly envy, soldiered through
repainting H on W.
Such can't be meant. Other dimensions
to their existences? No doubt.
But none improved what they slopped out
as tea. They've gone now, on their pensions
somewhere, paintbrush at last hung up,
crouched to the dregs of their last cup.

Which brings me to myself, revolving
such matters on a starlit beach
on Ireland's northern rim, and solving
none of my problems as I reach
perhaps my own half-way, at forty.
Pure romanticism, each sortie
risking its leap before the look
jells, has run into Life's left-hook
absurdly often. Once more home is
dwindled to little more than these
shoes I stand here in, where the sea's
belling as wind gets up, and foam is
whitening now to topple sheer.
There's plenty of the void round here.

But what I've journeyed to it out of
can't reclaim me. Visiting where
I "left home" from brings on no bout of
nostalgic oh-if-only: there
today, now stuck in mortgaged houses
staring across the rug at spouses
they married at nineteen because
a year of "going steady" was
sufficient for a blind society
subtly to put screws on, the kids
that I once played with flip their lids
or bear it, swallowing a variety
of tranquillising pills; sustain
hope with annual trips to Spain.

Flabbier now, they're yelling after
their own teenagers on the run
in parks where I found thrills and laughter:
like shrunk green teatrays in the sun
they look now, memory's suburban
Edens; and best not to disturb. In
shops, pubs, buses, when I'm among
them these days, both the old and young
shock me, pursed up, shut off, or showing

furtive hatreds, making me long
for Ireland's open talk and song,
wonder how I survived my growing.
I wondered then. My mother's frown
still wishes for me "settling down".

I've tried. The yearning that unsettles
began still earlier, cast its spell
when childhood's back-lawn cherry petals
one spring noon flutteringly fell
from swaying boughs to where I waited
with a cracked teacup and breath bated
to catch such as I could, and keep
for ever. After that night's sleep
already my pink hoard had withered;
rain pattered on dark laurel leaves
in a dimmed garden. What bereaves
all cherishing hurt my soul. I dithered
indoors with paltry toys . . . Next day
deep in woods flashed the brilliant jay.

That half-mile stretch of Epping Forest
around our first house, vaulting boughs
of oak, beech, hornbeam, where bird chorist-
ers thronged, sometimes a dozen cows
turned loose, and silver birches peeling
soft bark like paint, conferred a feeling
prelapsarian, pure and free.
Nine was the perfect age to be
I knew, just old enough for straying
without one's parents, not yet hit
by homework, tests. But then the writ
of adults intervened, conveying
me across London, stripped away
that whole first world, woods, friends and play.

So, Norwood; where, sent out for shopping,
I'd take a ball between my feet
and book in hand, and saunter, stopping

to trap a rebound. In our street
people considered thus combining
the two things odd; my mind was mining
the black depths of galactic space:
our island-earth, I read, a place
speck-like, lost, infinitesimal,
due to be swallowed by the sun;
life randomly from gas begun,
a sort of freak recurring decimal.
Perspective there on hacks who'd bore
at school of "what you're cut out for."

Also, the library held the ocean:
fascinated by frigate, barque,
galleon, longship, my emotion
hovered most round the *Cutty Sark*;
I travelled in imagination,
all voyages of exploration,
Frobisher, Cook, Magellan, Drake;
and fought with Grenville, Nelson, Blake;
and in Marryat's books through pouring
suburban indoor afternoons
adventured tropic blue lagoons;
I clung to wind-tossed park trees roaring
"Eternal Father, strong to save,
Whose arm doth bind the mighty wave."

No clues nor reason then for guessing
vagaries bringing me to stand
where waves are mightily depressing
this winter on Portstewart strand.
Our setting-forth's exhilaration
can never tell its destination;
nor can what's reached call back and warn
the younger self of not-yet-born
defeats and pains. That ghost still living,
a phosphorescence of the tide,
in me here as I walk beside
the North Atlantic's not forgiving

my failure to resolve distress.
Nor I him his ingenuousness.

And no, I never joined the navy;
but knew it through the school cadets:
hammock-slung mess-deck, awful gravy,
foul "heads", illicit cigarettes
on HMS *Dido* and *Bermuda*.
Sailors' conversation was cruder
than in books; and it seemed to be
the case they hardly got to sea
at all, that 'fifties Home Fleet rotting
greyly in Portsmouth, Devonport;
till mothballed, scrapped, or sometimes bought
by Turks and such. I liked the yachting.
But not the whole thing's purpose: war.
Also, my eyesight was too poor.

As a child I had one recurring
nightmare in which I'd stayed out late
on playing-fields; and no breeze stirring.
Suddenly clouds would dissipate
as froth, the goalposts wriggled sliding
beneath the ground like worms, and gliding
from under every bush a man
and girl fled shrieking. And I ran:
over the plain huge crabs were making
towards me; far roofs shrank away;
I looked back – that obscene array
of claws and jaws neared . . . I fell . . . waking.
The roses on my curtains wore
crueller faces than before.

But at sixteen I ran out training
each winter night, past lit shops, rows
of residential windows staining
the dark with brilliant cameos;
until the last built road ascending
the tilt of downs; to halt, breath rending

my chest. Violet burned the night
above South London on the right;
remote stars' harsh ignition studded
black wastes above. I leaned to cool
within a humming lamp-post's pool
of frail light, while my heart still thudded;
then dropped into a homeward track;
knowing one day I'd not turn back.

And so, I walked out on my schooling
in mid-term; others thought me mad.
Then left home. And I wasn't fooling:
intent, excited, frightened, had
outgrown the adolescent years of
make-believe in the park, the tears of
first love, talk about sex, God, cars,
and sunlight on the handlebars
cycling to Keston. I'd the notion
I must test out what Conrad meant,
"In the destructive element
immerse," and cast upon life's ocean
discover if I'd sink or swim.
I found myself out on a limb.

"SINGEL ROOM GENT NR SHOPS. BUS, STACION
1 MIN, US BATH" on boards outside
newsagents led to education
different from any school had tried:
rickety chair, bowl-fire, asthmatic
washbasin in those slant-roofed attic
rooms where if I sat up in bed
forgetfully I'd bang my head;
others' intimate sounds through meagre
partitions; furtive landing-smiles;
cracked front-steps spilling bottles; miles
of strange streets all round I was eager
to roam, where boughs in lamplight cast
black beams of shadow as I passed.

Cramped boxes, from imagination
wringing what it might have of song,
where I read, dreamed, yearned: my conflation
of life's wonders congealed to long
novel-drafts; I found I'd outgrown all
fast as written; have long since thrown all
that away; but never what went
into its making. One could rent
in 'fifty-eight for two pounds weekly
a window with a piercing view
beneath Parnassian eaves. And who,
looking, I'd wonder, at that bleakly
glinting pane from the drab street guessed
who lived there, rapturous, distressed?

Meanwhile, I earned my bread and butter
in offices, kitchens, bookshops; through
my bloodstream London's twilight mutter
insinuated: Waterloo
Station's cavernous rush-hour; whisper
of escalators; cash-tills' crisper
echoings; news cried; scraps of jazz
from gratings; starlings twittering as
each dusk in millions they settled
on ashen roofs along the Strand.
I changed jobs often, which made bland
Personnel Managers rather nettled:
"You've been a drifter, it would seem."
They'd tell me of their pension-scheme.

Summer 1981

Green drumlins swept delectably with light,
pegged by kempt farms, an old truncated tower;
sheep belly-deep, rose-gardens, dappled lanes
flowering hedgerow and July's quenched whin.

"Only two snows this century round here . . ."
Such rich confection seems life's natural ground,
no transient conjuring. Stone eagles gaze
at the Mournes' far serrations, wilderness

reduced to décor. Just one pool reflects
some troubling essence dark beyond thin air . . .
Till sign-stuck petrol stations, country shops
coagulate past our windscreen to Belfast.

Funnelled down Ormeau Road we hit the blitz,
or what's left outcropped: gable-ends, gapped streets
leprous with scrawled SMASH H-BLOCKS, FTQ,
RUC MURDERERS; black lamp-post flags

for the hunger-strikers. Then, abruptly, THIS
IS UVF TERRITORY, red white blue . . .
The steel-engirded city-centre shops
are tricked with royal wedding souvenirs.

Clear above all Cave Hill, where in high grass
bloom coloured galaxies perennial
since ice inched sculpting this terrain. Brief foam
on the black welter out of which all comes.

A Derry Farm

A five-mile reach of pasture elevated
into June and larksong, strewn with reeds,
purple orchid and gold-smouldering whin.
The clipping-shed's oil-fuelled generator
rackets on the skyline, till we dip
losing it for the trickle of brook water
through boulders, with a trodden path that leads
to the escarpment's fenced top. Congregated
against the foot below woods ripple green,
as if a garment that the farm's let slip.

Ewes break down there when they take a notion.
You drive right round by road to fetch them back,
that land's no use. But yours to the stone wall
faint as a thread. Beyond the railway track
reticulated fen bordered by yellow
strand curves to the Point and squat Martello
Tower, where the Foyle turns into ocean
glittering like a harp, about it curled
cloud-soft a lambent arm of Donegal.
You might suppose you'd risen above the world;

at least, compared with what you left for it,
that this world's nearer something we all dream
of, as if exiled from. Not heaven, exactly –
a whirr along the cliffs and sudden scream
as gulls mob a marauder, pull us round;
and as we circuit back, matter-of-factly
you show an empty buzzards' nest the crows
got at last week; and skewed upon the ground
a dead sheep rots, its groin a bloodied pit,
flies crawling from void eye-holes down black nose.

You heave it off the precipice, stench whooshes
up and wool-shreds flutter to the grass.
In fallen drystone that walled tiny fields
and rubbled cottages, a hungrier past

obtrudes its lineaments. Eased now by cars
and subsidies life at this height, where bushes
grow flinching from what the Atlantic wields
in winter, when snow drifts and torrents roar,
still takes the brunt. But closer to that core
our days would bite to; fitted to a vast

sky's indifferent shifts of grey or blue
subduing all to unity we guess
or part recall as ours back somewhere when
we did not know time moved, that growing older
lost the vision, left us settling wryly
to sort its fragments – down here, where again,
in my mind's lens, stray lamb across your shoulder,
you trudge broad undulations for its ewe;
outlined on the far horizon Islay
rising lucidly from changelessness.

A Winter's Tale

Woodpigeons brooding in a sunlit glade.
From the hollow-rooted tree by the green pond
sudden to glimpse a dragonfly's blue blade
glitter then gone; day-dreams and water-sound;

and "such a day tomorrow as today,
and to be boy eternal". Other weather,
tobogganing-time, sharp autumn, foaming may,
varying, drew rich pattern's threads together.

Like stories whose *And then? . . . And then? . . .* returned
to *Safe home round the fireside . . .* Where, December
pulping lawn past the glass as when I learned
of light-years-distant nebulae, I remember

how feeling inside so much so far and bright,
clockwork-routine in long continuance,
seemed confirmation then, like bed each night,
not solitude terrorized by wastes of chance.

So what changed? Rather, how? Yes, adolescence
tuning the world out of itself, and no
hint of idealism's corrosive essence.
But more, it's realizing life's cyclic show

cherishes only foliage, not leaf.
Still this drab winter's ceremonious.
Though eyes too young to know the vision brief
don't need estrangement's words to gloss it thus.

Cushendun

I stare at the whole contraption:
stone bridge, hotels on the quay,
crescent of strand, boats, sea.
That place one has always sought, a
miraculous refraction
above its shimmering water.

As if just off the map.
Sweeps of glen when I turn;
trees escort the burn.
In the cottaged street, a shop.
Tentatively I post
a card, feel like a ghost.

Of course, all's real enough,
rock-firm as its sandstone caves.
Talk I join in the bar
is travel, jobs, A-level stuff;
as also no doubt on that far
Scottish coast across gilded waves

like yet another dimension
tranquilly outlined. The era
of Gaelic and turf and flax
is over, however its aura
persists, or we pay no attention
to TV news at our backs.

The hotel Family Night's
packed tourists and locals in.
The area's Irish class
presents disco-dancing: mites
gyrate to anywhere-noise;
new steps, old discipline.

Last whiskeys. Kathy, Sinead,
three farmers. "I want more

than the life here." "Protestants
won't come these years, they're afraid."
"That murder . . ." Dark elements
outside. Staff sweep the floor.

At breakfast, feeling rough,
I gaze out at the ocean
through glass, its assuaging motion
cradles the headland. Enough
stir in its time to knock
that arch clean through black rock.

I read in the morning papers
of bombings, disasters, crisis,
states' and their foes' mad capers.
Nowhere a paradise is
untainted. That blue Moyle screens
"our" nuclear submarines.

Then, history's chill seep:
although by trick of the light
belying all connection,
slopes ravelling streams and sheep
have borne famine and eviction,
pogroms, the '98.

That ruin along the shore,
ivied and picturesque,
is Castle Carra where
the MacDonnells, beaten by
him at Red Bay and Glenshesk
lured Shane O'Neill to die,

cut down after the feast;
then gave his head to the Queen.
Only a clansmen's putsch, a
few years and the Sasanach seized
all Ulster. Today between
kempt hedges dripping fuchsia

the Mobile Library lurches;
doorstep milk's fetched in.
Though no-one was astounded
when a British frigate landed
a party conducting searches
last week. Old discipline.

Fragile in time and place
on this planet our heuristic
aggrandisements may blow
life off or waste through slow
entropy, a grace
note, anachronistic,

these Arcadian fragments stake
irrefutably green claim
to a world that keeps some room
for images we make:
waters for heart's retroflexion,
contours shaping direction.

Birth Day

1

The waters have broken. Now your body's slow
convulsions irreversibly begin.
Packing, I finger-lift a slat of blind:
the low roofs sleep, tree-traceries
rising like dreams, faint watermarks on night.

2

Admission seems a languid dream
of birth inverted: sunken entry lipped
with flexing doors, a lift ascending through
dormant entrails to the labour ward . . .
My overshoes squeak on aseptic floor
around this candid trolley-bed where you
are laid; dawn greying past your pane.

3

You are subdued to process,
an intravenous drip tamped in your wrist;
divested of your clothes, belongings, watch,
almost of me beside you. Shifts
of nurses, midwives, come and go, abstracting
to ink on paper your identity;
while, irrevocable hourglass,
above you the translucent glucose-drip-bag
decanting sheds its luminosity.
You cry "I can't bear this" as yet again
the shark's-tooth jag of a contraction shows
ticking through the monitoring-machine.
Like metering needles frail gold earrings shaking.

4

"Bear down . . ." Your palm grips mine,
your body opening like petals and

ah! the bloodied head emerging,
a wriggled slither and, suspended there
as if a tiny astronaut connected
by the umbilical's rich purple coil
to life-support, "You have a son."
Steel cuts the link. Adrift
– oh lost the dark close amniotic warmth! –
a huge convulsion gasps wide world's thin air.
Brute fact miraculously borne.

5

The fallen world rolls over into night.
Two army vehicles splash through lamplit rain,
miniskirts throng a disco. Things
ongoing register again.
My "Goodnight" left you hazed on a ward bed;
and you, our Rory, ankle name-tagged, parked
one in a row of wheeled transparent cots:
beautiful accident, success
in lieu of whose unique incipience
like failed intentions cells in millions died.
You are fallen on history's brink. Unthinkable,
"one bomb no bigger than a cricket ball"
could shrivel Belfast, gunmen, parents, all
who have been babies. Meanwhile
I follow in the wake of my own shoes
with doubled vision childhood paths among
green forest, still the singular
configuration of my favourite beech;
my first-loved books reopening their wings;
half-conscious at a crossing I come to,
carry myself with novel care,
a cup trembling to overbrim.
Frail lighted streets diverge into wet dark.
The world rolls hurtling you beyond my sight.

Whirligig

for Rory

Headline-hopping through racial wars,
strikes, drug-scares, fashions, cricket scores,
I've missed this morning build its high
never-to-be-repeated sky.
I let the Sunday papers drop,
and watch my child pump at his top,
regenerating spin; it hums,
successively each colour comes
to perfect circle, blurs, then dies;
usurped by what next clarifies.

An accelerated paradigm
of history's images: each time
form coheres, illusory stasis,
some gathering shade within displaces
it. New definitions break.
Sunk fragments gleam, as in a lake.
No refinement of infrared
photography conjures back the dead;
yet lingering perturbation floats
from buried centuries spectral notes.

A goblet, say, struck by a spoon
one leisurely late afternoon
by the Garonne. Immaculate
around spreads the matured estate,
tended by slaves: woods, ponds, herds, plough;
once more ripe apples weight the bough;
grape-clusters mirrored in the stream,
reeds, banks, are sealed there as in dream.
What if Germans have crossed the Rhine?
He raps again, commands more wine.

Bangled barbarians can't stampede
law, legions, libraries. All's greed
and glitter back in Rome; but here

carts trundle straight roads purged of fear.
Later than common sense can know.
Too near the day his son will go
to Bordeaux, and just not return;
Goths seize these lands, his villa burn.
So much gone. So much yet to come.
Give it a whirl, and let it hum.

Pining towards a harmony
that earth-bent eyes can never see,
the medieval field of folk
scatter their seed, past beech and oak,
backing towards us, looking back
on infants laid down in their track;
in time, all falling into place.
Shrovings, maypoles, tabors, lace;
beyond night's huddled eaves, wild beasts,
the Fiend with reap-hook, witching feasts.

They labour, revel, stink; recoil
craving abstraction, ritual,
in frozen surge of stone entomb
space incensed as God's ante-room.
Life is a scrabbling at greased rungs
between the Pit and choiring tongues
of angels. Earthly state's ordained,
those who mince in silk have gained
nothing of Heaven. From Traitor's Gate
void sockets quiz a fled soul's fate.

Dissolve again, quicken the pace,
hazard frail caravels to trace
the planet round, chart silences
blanched by combers. Metastases
of trade and power, the suffrage, shares,
din of machines, dispel dark fears:
ancestral spires' quaint maquillage
embellishes a railway age.

Safe as houses. Shires repeat
a trance of cumulus and wheat.

The earth's a project, a resource.
Uncloistered, the starched sahib tours
his district on an elephant;
iron ideals, box-files, and plant
reduce bow-cultures, fever-zones
to cushion laurelled English lawns
where daguerreotypes they posed for frame
pride braced in fashions new to them;
remote from basements where the soul
gestates revenge, cast out, unwhole.

Twelve chimes. A radiant cab; the driver
dozing above, homeward . . . and over
the brink of 1900, new
century opening, landslide. Two
by two those twined in Lover's Lane
are severed. Bluebells pool again,
but shellholes pool in the morass
where he disintegrates. A pause,
jazz, joy-rides, screen-dreams. It renews,
sifts gold from ashes of gassed Jews.

Ramps dizzying on, all now replaced
only by aggregating waste:
bombed villages, dustbowl, dumped foodstocks,
poisoned estuaries, tower blocks.
Dialled wires click, the wilderness
expands. Wrong number. Wrong address,
Deathwish aerosolled on the wall.
Aircraft show homecomers sprawl
they never chose; space-probes beam back
a coloured bubble lost on black.

Sad retrospect! Horizon gone
for ever . . . Oh, but once upon
a time, a track, half-knowing why,

his universe what met his eye,
something in us reared to walk stark
upright, a staggering landmark!
Galactic spindrift fertilised
miracle we've destabilised
to cities where the human heart
is sick, and people lie a part.

While guardian angel submarines
patrol pre-Cambrian capes. Machines
twinkle in bunkers, warning lights
monitor girdling satellites.
"200 50-megaton
nukes on the Russians, and we've won.
They're more exposed, except for mere
biological continuance. Here
the industrial fabric will survive,
control, the President alive . . ."

A top lies toppled on the floor.
Bored with it, calling from the door,
my son, you'll play another day.
The spokesman from the USA
fades on the screen, unreal beside
our here and now, noon sun outside
immune to slipstream, hung there staid
and homely as this room's lampshade.
I walk you out, we pass a brown
horse, grassed lane lifts us beyond town.

Through your delight I relive grace
notes squandering in this casual place:
petal, hedge-dapple, shade unfurled
on gleaming slope; world within world.
Pouring me back to what might be
our ancestor at gate or tree
inwrought to such inheritance,
trusting its dynasties of chance.

May they enfold you. Some day too,
somewhere, your children after you.

Over the hills and far away
flickers reiteration of May;
essential green here immanent
restores intact all we once meant.
Let none loose counterwise the power
at the universe's core,
the nuclear blossom's candid white,
all history vanishing in light.
In quasar spectra a redshift
measures lights out. We catch the drift.

No strength in me, your fragile shield,
can salvage Eden in a field.
Gossamer flutters what had wings;
a beak stabs; yet another wrings
pure arias from this underplot
to large design. Leaves whisper what,
like metaphor, to truth refracts
meanings plain speech makes inexact.
Ours for the asking, as years take
us, circles widen, bubbles break.

On Farthing Downs

Through seas of grass you run
ecstatic at what's given;
light-soused blue above
what you might think the glens
last week at Cushendun,
but is, an airflight thence,
Coulsdon downland's curve
fitting a Surrey heaven.
I compose you in a frame
of background still the same

as I grew up with: Sunday
walks, then from the school
I got translated to
friends living hereabouts.
I asked, invited one day
to tea and scones, "So that's
your mum?" A pause, then "No,
our servant." Like a fool
I flushed, plucked at my trousers.
Still those copious houses

are anchored along valleys
where car-wheels scrunch on gravel
meandering past mature
cypress and flowerbeds.
A world of golf and rallies
whose fathers lolled in tweeds
at wide french windows sure
of providence as civil
as their doucely shrugging day;
and saw no close of play.

As each man's out, replace
the bails, call the next.
In panelled calm heirs ripened
to an honours roll

remote from wilderness
of polity or soul.
Suez, Strikes, Sex, happened,
foxing a set text
that knew what England's for,
sandcastles round her shore.

Nearly three decades' lapse
since I last trod this chalk
convexity, took in
vistas hard to call
home now my inner map's
clouded by the pall
of Ireland in between:
changed county-shapes, the bulk
of mountain ranges where
all glitters in salt air.

I press down with my thumb
and snap! your photograph
is taken where, my son,
you've never been before.
Where still the insects thrum,
minute ephemera
of eternal summer one
parches after, half
believing it the place
where its state of grace

descended long ago:
cork-tips and cherryade,
a bicycle wheel ticking;
to lie balancing the sun
on raised knee under slow
sky-passages; or run
for running, or else kicking
a ball about. I shade
my eyes at that red kite
so motionless it might

be 1956's
still high in homeless blue.
For which I cut adrift.
As you may, from your place,
in time, that meanwhile fixes
contours we can't efface,
histories we've left,
heart-deep: for me, this view,
and luxury flotillas
of dozing greenbelt villas.

That taught me to call dinner
lunch, and knew the score.
Not even my own streets –
what ambiguities
made me as a beginner
find charms of paradise
dressing people I thought twits!
A lacquered enclave for
composure entertained
to hear itself arraigned.

Playing Armstrong's *Tin Roof Blues*
I imagined negro faces
under a full moon,
battered instruments
letting their night suffuse
subtopian lineaments,
like lava thrilling down,
shooting-star-burn traces
along this ridge, pure jet
of trumpet, clarinet.

Child's play. Put aside.
Revisitant, I laugh:
all looks so as-it-was
yet can't be, a time-warp
denying that it's died;
to your play blank, a drop

of backcloth weightless as
in squares of photograph
one day you'll inherit.
Fated not to share it.

from *"A Father's Tale"*

1. *"Daddy Mend It"*

Summer sealed the garden as you played,
gentle with petals, smiled at the black cat
lapping milk you poured. Green habitat
intact against whatever edge of shade.

One fallen leaf on the lawn's grass. You ran
and tried to put it back on its low bough;
then said "Daddy mend it", knowing how
I've fixed a light, your broken top, toy van,

and gave me it trusting that yet again
I'd make all right. And found that wasn't true,
there is no trick of screwdriver or glue
for growing things; but how could I explain?

Or now. Since mad October's massive fall
whirling you over salt estranging sea.
Hail-scourged in dark yearns the stripped weeping tree
precarious greenness hints and can't forestall.

2. *Lullaby*

Child, so beautiful
in repose,
tousled silk hair,
pale snub of nose

gently exhaling,
nails pearl-clear
on small fingers curled
round your teddy bear;

outside your cot,
and moonlit room,
spread fens of exile
from what meant "home".

Where I stare at the moon,
as if love might,
a pulley-rope drawn
by your feather-fate

over it, toss
me to you. Sleep
my darling, nor ever
dream that I weep.

But when from mists
wreathing you forms,
bent to your slumber
a ghost in your dreams,

assuaging your core –
hearth's flickering fire,
a hug when you fall,
guiding hand on the stair,

first friends, places, ball
beneath trees, river, town,
Pates Lane ponies;
all whirled back and gone

as if but a dream –
O, should you stir,
reach up to kiss
and meet thin air,

those purest blue
eyes would know
the intruder not
my vanished shadow

but the upstart world
shrilling your soul,
and cry to dream
of all made whole

again, as before
its madness threw
the terrible switch
abducting you.

I dandle shoes scuffed
with your toddler-fun:
one day, retreading
their steps, my son

you'll discover clear
of what spells it dead,
like Donegal
or Benbane Head

truth endures,
patient to bless
trust in its slopes,
its fabulous

peaks restoring
all lost ground,
reknit the whole
horizon round.

CHRISTMAS 1983

6. *Tyrolean Retrospect*

Will he remember this? we wondered. In
your pushchair from the Hahnenkamm you stare:
distant peaks like blossom spike clear air
that tinkles cowbells, burnishes your skin.

I turn the page: dirndl and lederhosen.
wrought iron shop-signs, flowering balconies,
falls of green pasture draped with Alpine trees;
the Golden Roof; small figures on the frozen

tongue of the Grossglockner glacier; ledged
chunks of schloss from the Imperial cake;
a Salzburg palace mirrored in blue lake.
All sifted to this album. Double-edged,

the foreignness – north meaning Germany;
bitte and *danke* – was entrancing fable
owed no living duty, so destabil-
izing us because it set us free

of all except ourselves, home-truths beyond
what the camera framed. For you, not knowing
where you were, or where we might be going,
"abroad" just added on to native ground.

Innocent of history, you crawl
the Hofburg ballroom's marble floor as if
at playgroup, past idealized Habsburgs stiff
in antique finery upon the wall.

"One day we will come back to stand again
here on the Panoramaweg," we said.
What she's done since has knocked that on the head.
All family perspectives down the drain,

may one, which as our cablecar dipped, fed
your gaze, persist; against life's ugliness
immunize your soul. Who could not guess
such exaltation hung by a mere thread.

7. *For My Son*

Again May's blossom foaming past,
indifferent to what since last

time round has exiled me from all
attunement to its seasonal
bag of tricks. A pavement tree
lopped back last winter helplessly
conjures from black stumps a dance
of fresh leaves; daisies take their chance
in galaxies; red blooms adorn
municipally-tended lawn.
Each form unique, and rooted here.
Replaced by much the same next year.
  New pushchairs trundle past the sea
here in your place, my son. Since she
revoked your birthright, all I'd share
with you squanders against my stare,
falling to ashes. You are gone.
Uselessly spring's show goes on.
  Drawn by its weather to this coast
families sprawl or stroll. A ghost
infiltrating, I retrace
old steps, as if once more your face
might bob past on the carousel.
One blink, all magically well
again . . . An empty horse glides round.
And round. And over there the sound
of laughter from the Slippery Dip.
Far out, incurious, a ship
pointing away from Ireland, buoyed
on a blue flux beneath blue void.
  I walk again this curve of strand,
a shine of wet on firm gold sand
blanked by 500 tides since you
knelt watching Daddy as I drew
a little boy, incised your name:
RORY WAS HERE. Here looks the same:
dunes, headlands, ocean charged with light
as then, rippling to its long white
ribbon of foam, where bubbles break
in millions for each breath I take.
Standing on its edge I stare

at the expanse of water where
ceaselessly varying one theme
waves crest and lapse; a cosmic dream
wherein what shaped our selves first stirred,
progenitive subsentient curd;
then instinct tipped with jaws, routine
rendings and matings, submarine
aeons never asking why;
crawling at last beneath the sky
beyond which constellations spin,
their chemistry life's origin.
  Innumerable stars and sperm . . .
Interrogation can't confirm
my almost-faith that you were meant,
no sport of chance, but heaven-sent;
and yet, as sandgrains on a plate
stimulated to vibrate
by sweet notes from a violin
gather to a pattern in
the nodal lines, so when I hold
you in my arms next will the cold
welter of space-time reshape
to lucid focus, stellarscape
vindicated in the rays
of love that interlock our gaze.
  As fourteen days ago: again
a boat across to Scotland, then
the night-train dreaming southward to
ticking wheels, a shave at Crewe,
and halting curve through the spoiled heart
of England as commuters start
their workday. Scented typists cram
the carriage into Nottingham,
spill dispersing; Lincolnshire
expands monotonously. Dear
child, lost to the sea-surge, light
on soaring headlands, wheeling flight
of gulls, Glenarriff's waterfalls.
I greet you within office walls

among Probation Service staff.
She sits and glowers, while you laugh
with joy to find a swivel chair
"a roundabout. Daddy sit there."
  All now depends upon the Court.
The Welfare Officer's report
assesses your "best interests
are served best" if the Law invests
custody in me; although
she'll argue as the "status quo"
what she's brought you to; presume
the "mother's right" must overcome.
  Rory, all your future ought
to be pleads fate may not abort
its sunrises on mutual hopes,
cloth spread for three on picnic slopes
where insects thrum, your basic right
to childhood's freedom and delight
beneath the overarching love
of parents intertwined above.
That world, like a baby seal
lifting its eyes in mute appeal
against the club, knows no redress;
and is crushed into wilderness.
  I lift you to the windowsill
to watch the world go by, and thrill
as round my shoulder your small arm
curls gently. Child, she cannot harm
our bond, bright gold that will not rust
hooping our two souls in trust.
  With me on that "access" day
was Dermot, joining in our play.
Strange ravellings of bittersweet
chance and change and choice complete
inscrutable design in our
conjunction in that Lincoln hour,
three generations grouped to look
at pictures in a storybook.
  South-east Leinster is still thick

with Nolans. As when, famine-sick
they crawled the bohereens scrabbling for
raw turnips, died of scurvy or
the bloody-flux – grandchildren to
the famous Boys of Wexford who
rose in the '98 until
massacred at Vinegar Hill.
I can't know whether Patrick wept
for the once-proud Ó Nualláin sept
deGaelicised, dispossessed, denied
subsistence. The green countryside
of 1847 stank
of corpses. Slowly Ireland sank
astern. By exile he survived;
enlisted in Liverpool, arrived
in Bengal as a gunner, rose
to Quartermaster Sergeant, chose
an Irishwoman for his wife;
and died of cholera. A life
residual in fading ink
on scattered documents; a link
with a lost provenance. Nolans won
place in the Imperial sun
climbing rungs of the Raj, but still
ancestral Catholics. Until
you were born to Burmese days
in 1913, Dermot: blaze
of flowers, ricefields, the caress
of heat, whirls of stirred-rainbow dress,
lashed teak logs piloted downstream
past gilt pagodas. A charmed dream
of childhood, its still lotus pool
cancelled by England, boarding school,
Cambridge, and your regiment.
Thames holidays with punt and tent,
halcyon motoring Junes before
Europe's stormclouds broke in war –
the week a child was conceived.
You married Moyra, and believed

"it would work out". Her maiden name
Enright tells her forbears came
from Clare and Limerick. The frail
private tie, dwarfed by the scale
of the times' impersonal
coercions, broke. Before the fall
of France you were agreed the best
course, in the infant's interest,
would be at-birth adoption . . . Cared
for under skies where searchlights flared,
those London air-raid shelter nights
my earliest memory, droning flights
of bombers, bangs – yet innocent
of what that huge commotion meant,
unhorrified, intact, I grew
alternatively. And never knew,
through asphalt years inlaid with parks,
brash, dreamy, bookish, teenage sparks
of wondering what it's all about,
bedsitter drifting, finding out,
pain suffered, and pain caused, the real
eroding poster-paint ideal
to lay bare given world – that if
we open to it from the stiff
coiled self is patient to requite
us, use us as we sense it might.
Until, uprooted, grafted for
twelve years to this northern shore
where green glens trickle water, I
learned, following the death of my
adoptive father whom through sad
unmeant imbroglio I had
not seen since childhood, who had kept
the papers, details I thought swept
beyond retrieval, of my true
parentage. So I found you
in the London phonebook, kin
met for the first time: freckled skin,
bald, bespectacled . . . Among

your pot-plants, bric-a-brac, walls hung
with horsey Stubbs and Munnings prints
we've come to know each other since
that meeting, Dermot; and I have
lost, youthful Moyra's photograph.
And here in Ireland, as if some
hidden wheel at last had come
full circle since his ancestor
Patrick fled so long before,
native beside the River Bann:
Rory John Nolan Waterman.
  Till casually as one might swing
a stick she lopped that blossoming.
  My son, six footprints interwound
along this sand last year; you found
small shells I've kept, upon the beach
burnished by wind and water, each
the candid husk of some minute
brief living impulse. At the root
of all creation, stars and cells
proliferating, parallels
and mutations, cryptic hints
of pattern, random process, since
the original Big Bang
starting the entire shebang,
we crave some purpose, to confer
meaning upon our petty stir,
latecomers to a blue-green speck
of spinning planet we may wreck –
one madman's itchy fingertip,
or 40 cent computer chip
malfunctioning, to activate
our holocaust. And yet innate
gratuitous imperatives
by which our human nature lives –
so that as small seeds buried in
the earth respond to an unseen
light and striving upwards may
flower at last to unguessed day

the soul aspires – compel us. Laws
of physics cannot be the cause
of prisoner Kolbe's "Take me instead"
when one picked out for dying shed
tears for his family; to refute
the Nazis with an absolute
their ideology denies,
yet Auschwitz could not brutalise.
External circumstance can break
us; the response is ours to make.
   Art seeks to forge atoning sense
and shapeliness from violence
and hurt we may be powerless
in life to help. These lines confess
sheer impotence, as they complete
their formal pattern, to defeat
or solace discord which has ripped
you from your home and father, stripped
away known places, play and friends;
yet while it cannot make amends
for wrong endured, the poem sustains
truths life would void; by taking pains
composes our essential form,
inviolable through the storm.
   Unfathomable, transmitted through
quantum leaps we can't construe,
and multimillion flukes of chance
encounter, whim, and circumstance,
the force that moves the galaxies
shines now incarnate in your eyes,
specific in a soul's unique
flowering from birth to seek
fulfilment. Rory, far today
from where you've watched this ocean sway,
successive heaves and crestings each
toppling to froth washed from the beach
by the next breaker, trust the flow
of life's wave through you as you go
intensifying onward, bright

parabola beyond my sight
into the microchip and space-
culture future of our race.
May love, which science cannot spell,
by grace of which alone we quell
devouring impulses, attend
your great adventure to its end,
your gift according as it can
with the brief music which is man.
   And, in spite of everything,
mend, next time round, our broken spring.

Thoughts of Blaise Pascal in East Anglia

for Chris and Joan Speake

Suave Wroxham lawns mown to the water's edge.
In this flat county even rivers stand
still, or as good as. Reeds and sedge,
sun-dappled foliage, liquid sounds, expand

through winding miles of Broadland peace. We chug
past other launches, triangles of sail
for two hours, circle shallows dug
for peat in ancient times. A pint of ale,

then back to leafy Norwich cul-de-sacs
where television prattles: Mozambique
babies are boiled alive; Iraq's
bombed Gulf shipping; new Cruise Missile leak.

Lost in this corner of the universe . . .
"We play squash several evenings; jog." Me too,
guest of courtesies fearing no worse
than showers to spoil a garden barbecue;

sure of this man-made part of England where
no natural features, mountain, waterfall
rearing untamed and always there
measure our human lives as brief and small;

and on far, farmed horizon trees stand clear
at sunset, neutralising Pascal's sense
of Nature as *an infinite sphere*
the centre everywhere, no circumference.

Who knew as *useless, dubious*, Descartes
assembling life's traffic in appearances
from "cogito", setting mind apart
from world. For *man is bound to all he sees.*

All this visible universe only a drop
on the ample breast of nature, infinite
beyond where even imaginings stop.
No idea of ours approaches it.

Yet also: *Take a mite, its legs, veins, blood,*
drops in that blood. And see a new abyss
immense within the atom . . . A flood
sways us . . . The earth yields, voids craved certainties.

Full of itself, his vain and gaudy age
attended salons, cock-fights, or the shout
of Frondeurs. Blood flowed. Centre-stage,
an armoured Church cast bat-winged Jansen out.

Themes change. Now pickets and police replace
forgotten social turmoils. We debate
no longer God's "efficient grace",
but embryo-culture, votes, the Welfare State.

Or wearying of such matter, idle at
video-games: my joystick guides a "frog"
through the screen's hurtling "traffic" . . . Splat! . . .
The next one makes it, hops from log to log

across the river, dodging crocodiles;
and so on, till five lives are lost, and then
GAME OVER: YOUR SCORE . . . Well, it whiles
an hour away. I press, and start again.

Diversion soothes our miseries; yet it
is our worst misery, functioning to stop
us thinking of ourselves . . . We hit
a ball for points; chase hares. Until we drop.

Like one in prison, ignorant of what
his sentence is, who to secure repeal
has one hour, killing the time he's got
playing piquet! It is unnatural!

Discoverer of the syringe, calculus
and, asked by gamblers, of the laws of chance,
your clear mind discomposes us
into stark elements, as we advance

stupefied by our technology toward
perhaps the day its fires burst in blue air
above Thorpe Road or Hickling Broad;
and then the nuclear winter, everywhere . . .

Game over. And we never knew the score . . .
Meanwhile, the weather holds, six weeks of drought
have finished the roses off before
this year's GCE results are out

for parents sprawled on patios, conifer
secluding this from that house, who turn pages
of the *Sunday Times*. Bees stir
among Virginia creeper that assuages

this residential redbrick which somehow
displaced what greener impulses pursued,
never defined. Their children's now?
Uncertainty. Ennui. Inquietude . . .

Alone on Halvergate Marshes in a bleak
November twilight you can stand attuned
to bitterns booming, and the creak
of derelict windpumps, opening like a wound;

apparitions, cows and cattlegate
among the wetland's random clumps and spikes
of grass; a world still inchoate;
moonlight shuddering in drainage dykes.

Man is only a reed, the weakest thing
in nature; but a thinking reed, thereby
nobler than forces that may wring
the life from us; because we know we die.

In nature. Knowing it unfalsified
to a Cartesian mechanism we
might infer, but verified
upon our pulse experientially.

Pascal, the creaturely empiricist,
when Descartes claimed by reason vacuums
in nature could nowhere exist,
devised fit tests, observed, and did the sums.

But analysed this apple has no taste.
Heat is mere movement of small particles.
And you are, my good friends, replaced
by unconsenting stacks of molecules.

As lines, squares, cubes – or x, x^2, x^3 –
are different orders, similarly apart
are modes of knowing, to be grouped
as proper to the senses, reason, heart.

The heart has reasons reason does not know.
In us like rivers. *Rivers are moving roads*
that would take us where we want to go.
Even these torpid among Norfolk's Broads,

their names blunt Anglian, Bure, Yare, Ant, Thurne,
pragmatic villages where life enquires
means, not ends, moves taciturn,
flint churchtowers lacking visionary spires,

this afternoon's gold miles of stubble-field
proposing an accountant's universe
calculable in its yield –
all sense the sea, along which cars disperse.

We pause at Yarmouth: pier, bars, "Funland". Chris,
it's thirty years now since we first went to town
on the ideal; half-scared to kiss
real girls, bought for a laugh for half-a-crown

a six-inch rubber Jane Russell from a stall
that, squeezed, grew tits. While Joan, to reach a dance
you'd hitch wild miles through Donegal –
drunk melées in the ballrooms of romance.

You've settled here; your visitor, I live
in Ireland now. Willed quests? or quantum grace
notes, siftings from some cosmic sieve?
Our species a chance stanza flung on space?

In our perplexities our definition
and essential being. Pascal, great
physicist and mathematician,
inventor of the earliest calculat-

ing machine, gap-leaper, writing to Fermat,
Mathematics? I'd not step a metre for it;
thought's noblest practice; but only that,
having outstripped Europe, you ignore it.

For *our true study, man*. Until the pain
blossomed in your body, and you died.
The autopsy could not explain
the spiked belt next your skin reproving pride.

You'd scorn the glib ways we've conceptualised
ourselves since, breathing in like fuel-exhaust
narcotic jargons, desensitised
to our emotional truth. And built a vast

diversion-industry. The twig-limbed hosts
of famine gather on our screens, to set
full tables shuddering. Civic boasts
are scabbed with spreading slum graffiti . . . Yet

as now, car parked, we stare – blue flux, curved beach –
a childhood is re-entered. Here I came,
to Corton, magically each
August. Is that ship out there the same

as 1947's? Freedom far
as eye can reach . . . I clamber down, my hand
scrunching soft ochre cliffs; that are
the crumbling verge of smug recessive land.

Zugzwang

You'd be all right if you'd not got to move.
But it's your turn, the rules are you've to move.
But every legal move's a losing move.

Enemy forces whirl on looting jags,
slide into groove, and squinny down diags.
You'd be all right if you'd not got to move.

That blunder memory aborts – except
for smashed glass, bruises, blood-brushed clothes. You wept.
But it's your turn, the rules are you've to move.

The queen sidestepped your combo, pulled the rug
from under as you missed her *zwischenzug*.
But every legal move's a losing move.

Flexihour scotch, book-crawls, won't fend it off.
Your carefree early gambit dug this trough.
You'd be all right if you'd not got to move.

Or might pull through if you'd no known address,
just stray floors, lovers, chequered boundlessness.
But it's your turn, the rules are you've to move.

Mere pastime, not real life, this chess? No dice.
You're what you make, this mess no paradise.
But every legal move's a losing move.

Dawn's landscape, all squares snow-blanched. Spellbound, you've
no chance. White masses. Things will not improve.
You'd be all right if you'd not got to move.

In Memoriam Reggie Smith

1914-1985

It's like reaching to find no books on the shelf,
or turning with a smile to empty chair.
You trusted life as gift, gave of yourself.
Your postcard tells of projects in the air,
memoirs, a play, the Med. But the phone-call said you're dead.
How can I answer now when nothing's there?

"Pawn to King Four, old mate" . . . But I can't tip
the chess bits from the box to start again,
and hear that irksome ditty on your lip
as you cogitate, set traps, advance your men:
"By and by there'll be pie in the sky when you die."
Plus, for you, booze, cricket, talk, sex, poets, pen.

Up there, there's very few you'd not let in:
sociologists? cheats? bosses? pedants? – you'll
still separate the sinner from the sin,
living, some carped, by sentimental rule.
"Is there no-one Reggie hates?" "Can't he discriminate?"
You brought our best out, and were no-one's fool.

But I won't pretend you'd faith in any more
than human nature, though your own transcends
whatever is innate in any law
of physics . . . I've slipped gear to present tense,
a habit hard to kick – even after you got sick
you'd go anywhere for rugger, book-talk, friends.

Two strangers cast up on an island both
knew you, told your first novelizing wife.
From Wight to Perth to Dublin's Hill of Howth
we're all amputees still feeling you post-knife.
Farmers, writers, scientists; that Aussie tramp who turned up pissed
in Derry: "This fat Pom once saved my life."

But your epicentre was the BBC.
Bliss was it in that dawn when radio
"Features" bet on creativity,
not output, ratings, costings, admin . . . So,
Dylan's *Milk Wood*, Louis's *Tower* – and "The George". Until sour
compartmentalisers tidied up the show.

You kept that end up through the time you taught
our Coleraine students, scorning hacks who'd wall
poems behind analyses. You thought
teaching your "privilege" – and taught us all.
As, decades back, meeting classes, helping victims, till the Nazis
chased you from the Balkans at their fall.

Remember King's Cross? – scrambling to miss
a train, we sought the bar. Pints on our knees,
"'The moon shines bright. In such a night as this,'"
you quoted, "'wind did gently kiss the trees . . .
Let the sound of music creep in our ears . . .'" You took a deep
draught, "Sheer magic, everyone agrees;

but what time-serving academic guff
ignores is – why on earth did Shakespeare pick,
from the play's couples, them for lyric stuff? –
him a ponce and scrounger up to any trick,
her a traitor to her Dad and culture, thief, a bad
lot – delinquents both, ripe for the nick.

So what was going on in Shakespeare's head?
Had he forgotten they were shits? Or just,
wanting some uplift to send folk to bed,
didn't care? No, rather, you can trust
that, attuned to what is real, he knew even shits can feel
in such a night there's more to it than lust."

I glance out. Crewe. 5am. Right I write
you, mover, on the move; and to my kid;
the boat, this sleeper. You backed my doomed fight
(that drivelling judge) for custody, amid

your illness and tax-hash. Your card ends, "Soon more cash
to help." Reg, I owe you five hundred quid.

From your start spark-bright in dour depression Brum –
you'd all its ballads; and the Afghan Wars' –
you never lost, however far you'd come,
an axial sense of truth and a just cause.
The world's a smaller place, that can't look up and see your face.
Last week Earth missed a heartbeat: it was yours.

To the Island

Instead then, to the island: in this season
let the boat slip from laden mainland –
its supermarkets of words, entangling faces
lapse into cleansing greyness, shrug of water.
Somewhere ahead white cliffs so often seen
shimmering across blue sound in modulations
of prismatic light, the island
fragrant with wildflowers. But that was summer,
was love in different weather. Now it forms
as a mere coalescence; ventured on
is lustreless and monochrome.
Walk up beyond the few poor lights that cling
around Church Bay. Grass stirs,
and reeds chill in an unreflecting lake,
innocent of history – old massacre,
this fragment of a fort Drake's guns smashed down,
ruins of abandoned cottages.
See, you can prise from the landscape a handful
of flints – the Stone Age axe factory.
But countless birds for whom today means always
make these far headlands murmurous as beehives;
a flock of guillemots rises, like thunder.
The eye loses itself, as the sea clears –
until, out there, gleam Islay, Jura,
exposed unspoilt, the high peaks of the heart.

Lincoln Cathedral

It crowns the city's coil of traffic like
Christ knows how many tons of marzipan.
You pedal round its green verge on your trike
past lunchbreak typists sprawled to catch a tan.

And, inside the great contraption, stare
at stained glass, sculpted masonry, a cool
intricately proportioned scoop of air.
"This building's old, men made it beautiful,"

you say, preempting what books amplify;
then at a lit-up aisle depiction of
the Good Samaritan are puzzled why
you can't "put coins in so the people move".

Liking the place, you ask me what it's for.
Visitors shuffle, spouting French or Dutch.
Tills ting through the cathedral gift-shop door
dispensing teatowel souvenirs and such.

Part's roped off for a service going on;
you thrill to music from what seems to me
rites legendary as the dying swan,
sideshow to tourism, that cannot be

fitted to what's out there. Yet, petrified,
ritualised, in obsolete ornate
approximations, instincts that confide
our freedom from brute process congregate,

helpless against rebuff as when nailed to
the cross that's why these stones are here. We light
our candle, answer that makes sense to you,
a glow that goes on when we're out of sight.